THE
FRED FACTOR

HOW FRED THOMPSON MAY CHANGE
THE FACE OF THE '08 CAMPAIGN

by Steve Gill
Foreword by Congressman Zach Wamp

Music City News Publishing, Inc.
1616 Westgate Circle
Brentwood, TN 37027

Music City News Publishing, Inc.
1616 Westgate Circle
Brentwood, TN 37027

Produced and printed by Pop Color, Williston, VT
Cover design by ELBusa Creations, Phoenix, AZ
Cover photo by Carl Cox Photography, Rockville, MD

ISBN 0-9768737-1-0

ACKNOWLEDGEMENTS

First, thank you to Kathy, Patrick and Ryan for all of your love, support and encouragement in all that I do, including this book. I couldn't do what I do without you, and I love sharing it with you. Patrick and Ryan have often felt the pain of Mom's "red pen" correcting their school work; I now truly understand that experience myself. Special thanks, Kathy, and some degree of appreciation, for your efforts to cure my cavalier attitude towards the comma. 11.

Noelle Federico: thanks for prodding, pushing, pleading and pounding this book to fruition -- while running four companies, directing a radio show, raising Antonio, and shepherding all the other "kids" in our crew. You constantly amaze me with your efficiency, work load and perseverance.

Congressman Zach Wamp: Thanks, my friend, for adding your words to the book and for your leadership and passion in serving our country.

Jeff Jones: thanks for supporting this project and the Gill Media team financially and with your ideas and enthusiasm.

Trent Siebert: thanks for the contribution of ideas, research and background information.

Andrew, Leslie, Erin and all the other folks who help get the Steve Gill Show on the air and running smoothly: thanks for your patience and tolerance with the guy who decided to write a book in about four weeks.

To all the political backgrounders, players and insiders who contributed ideas, suggestions, deletions, and direction to the book. You all made the final product better, and I owe you one.

Finally, to Mom and Dad, your love, support, encouragement, confidence and prayers have always been more important than you could possibly know. You are the best.

Contents

Contents (con't)

Foreword

As the magnificent Capitol dome rises above the divisions that exist today in the United States Congress, so must the next President of the United States rise above the divisions across our great land to pull together the people of this nation to face the extraordinary challenges that we must address at home and abroad.

The political landscape does not favor the Republican Party as we head into the 2008 election. The Iraq war is necessary, but it is a political drag on our party going forward. The American people are somewhat restless as we struggle in Iraq and climb further in debt in the aftermath of September 11, 2001. They are looking for change, reform and strong leadership.

The important swing voters are searching for someone who can unite us and carry us through these dark and difficult days ahead. Each generation has someone who surfaces to rise above the fray and transcend the American political system. More and more, it seems that person is former U.S. Sen. Fred Dalton Thompson of Lawrenceburg, Tenn.

In the pages ahead, Steve Gill, host of one of the most influential radio talk shows in the South, explores the Fred Factor and how it shapes the 2008 presidential race. He examines who Fred Thompson is, the dynamics of the 2008 presidential election and where Fred Thompson stands on issues of importance to conservatives and constitutionalists.

Why Fred?

Fred Thompson personifies strength and trust – the two things the American people look for most in a president. He has a commanding presence, literally and figuratively. His stature and confidence reassure the people he serves, giving them the confidence that as we go forward he will lead us through whatever challenges we may face.

In eight years as a U.S. Senator, he established a consistent, conservative record. From strengthening national security to defending Second Amendment rights to protecting the sanctity of human life, Fred Thompson is the man who Republicans can rally around as their standard-bearer as we enter the 2008 presidential election.

Not a career politician, Fred Thompson has answered his country's call to serve again and again. He has not pursued the presidency, but it seems as though the presidency is pursuing him. He's highly electable, he's always been likeable. He's very comfortable in his own skin. He's serious minded, but he doesn't take himself too seriously. People are comfortable in the presence of Fred Thompson, whether on a movie set or the Senate floor.

Why now?

Recently I organized a meeting for Republican Members of the U.S. Congress, who had expressed a desire to meet with Fred Thompson and hear his views on a possible presidential campaign. About 60 House Republicans gathered one afternoon, just off the Capitol campus to spend an hour with this unique American. During that session, he was very transparent as he shared who he is, his life, the highs and lows, his deep held beliefs and the way we need to approach the many challenges our country faces today.

These mostly conservative Members of Congress said to Fred Thompson that he was presidential, and he is. They told him that he was electable, and he is. They said they hoped he would seek the presidency because the current Republican field, while filled with good and decent people, is not captivating the imagination of the American people or exciting the base of the Grand Old Party.

The belief among many in the House of Representatives is that if we as a party do not nominate someone who transcends politics and rises above the two parties, then the prospect of a Republican being elected in 2008 is not good. The cycle favors the Democratic Party, unless the likes of Fred Thompson seeks the presidency. We need a candidate who adheres to conservative principles with strong federalist beliefs in the role of the government and how freedom can and should work in America. Fred Thompson will be that candidate.

In this engaging book, you'll discover why Steve Gill is the Talk of Tennessee and why talk about the Fred Factor is spreading across the country. This is a worthwhile read about a worthwhile subject and a man who just may be the Republican Party's answer in the 2008 presidential race.

In his first movie role, Fred Thompson played himself as the prosecutor in the movie *Marie*, and in every role he's played on television, the movies and in real life ever since, he simply plays himself. He plays roles in which he's comfortable, in command and in control with a strong voice that people take seriously.

Some people call it charisma, in politics they call it gravitas, but in Tennessee, it's just plain old confidence. Fred Thompson knows who he is, where he came from and where we as a nation, must go together.

I had the privilege of serving alongside Fred Thompson for eight years while he served our state and our nation with distinction in the U.S. Senate. I wholeheartedly endorse his potential candidacy for president. Fred Thompson just may be the one to rise above the fray and unite the American people once again. I urge all conservatives, independents, Reagan Democrats and fair-minded Americans to give Fred Thompson a hard look as we move forward in the days ahead to consider our choices and elect the next leader of the free world.

U.S. Congressman Zach Wamp
Representing Tennessee's Third District

Introduction

HILLARY VERSUS FRED, 1974

The year is 1974. A nation gripped by a Presidential scandal that has rocked the very foundations of the political structure pays little heed to two young lawyers who are minor players in the drama, which is unfolding. These two attorneys are on opposite sides of the political and ideological divide, and no one at the time would suspect that they might eventually face one another in a battle with even bigger stakes. That "Watergate" investigation, which ultimately led to the resignation of one President, may have also begun a path to the Inauguration of one of those two young lawyers as the nation's next President.

Hillary Rodham was a recent Yale Law School graduate when she joined the impeachment inquiry staff advising the House Judiciary Committee in its investigation of the corruption and deceit surrounding a break-in at the Democratic National Committee headquarters. Hillary adopted her liberal ideological bent as an undergraduate at Wellesley, where she participated in campus anti-war demonstrations, defended the Black Panthers, and even worked in the law offices of one of the Black Panther's lawyers, Robert Treuhaft, a former communist.

Ever the political opportunist, Hillary had been elected President of the college's chapter of the Young Republicans before "seeing the light." As a senior she was elected President of the Wellesley student government then parlayed that position into a platform to denounce the Vietnam War at her graduation ceremonies in 1969. Her graduation became an effective "coming out" party for the politically ambitious liberal when *Life* magazine wrote a glowing article about her speech. Hillary pursued a liberal activist career at Yale Law School, including campaigning for George McGovern in his ill-fated

1972 Presidential campaign, and spent a brief period at the Children's Defense Fund before assuming her role in the Watergate proceedings.[1] She also apparently pursued, successfully, the man who would be our 42nd President of the United States, William Jefferson Clinton.

Fred Dalton Thompson took a dramatically different path to the Watergate hearings, and ultimately played a much larger role than Hillary. Thompson, a wise-beyond his years southern conservative Republican, was armed with an undergraduate degree from Memphis State University and a law degree from prestigious Vanderbilt University when he became co-Chief Counsel to the Senate Watergate Committee. He also brought three years of experience as an assistant U.S. Attorney to the table.

Thompson also worked in the 1972 election cycle, albeit more successfully and at a higher level of responsibility than Rodham. He'd also served as manager of Senator Howard Baker's successful 1972 re-election campaign.

Thompson drew on his prosecutorial background in helping to develop lines of inquiry into the political conspiracy and crimes surrounding the Watergate break-in, including Baker's historic line of Watergate questioning –"What did the President know, and when did he know it?" which may have led directly to the downfall of President Richard Nixon. Thompson briefly found himself in the spotlight, as the young counsel's probing questioning of Nixon aide Alexander Butterfield led to the revelation of the existence of listening devices in the Oval Office, resulting in the discovery of the infamous "Nixon tapes."

Few, if any, at the time would have expected these two to emerge as primary contenders for the Presidency three decades

---

1   *The Children's Defense Fund was founded in 1973 by liberal activist Marian Wright Edelman, who has been described as Hillary Clinton's "closest sister and ideological soulmate." The organization remains active today under the leadership of Edelman. www.childrensdefense.org.*

later. Yet, the stars seem to be aligning in a way which underscores the fact that politics not only produces some strange bedfellows, but also interesting and unexpected match-ups.

CAN ANYBODY BEAT HILLARY IN 2008?

DEMOCRATS?

Senator Hillary Rodham Clinton clearly faces a tougher than expected Democratic Party primary, particularly with the unexpected emergence of Senator Barack Obama as a well-funded, charismatic rival. Former Sen. John Edwards enjoys strong financial backing and status as the only "Southerner" in the Democrat field. However, most political prognosticators believe Clinton is still the odds on favorite to win her party's nomination, largely because so many delegates to the Democrat's convention will come from the ranks of those who owe their political allegiance to the Clintons.

What are her primary political assets? Certainly, former President Bill Clinton himself may be the biggest – an asset that is insurmountable by any other Democrat candidate. But as the nation saw throughout Clinton's term of office, former President Clinton can also be a huge political liability. That said, there are other assets on her political ledger sheet.

The big money donors and fundraisers are in Hillary's column with the full apparatus of the Bill Clinton financial machine at her disposal. The A-team political operatives are in Hillary's column, in part due to loyalty and past service and in part due to their fear of publicly attracting the ire of either Clinton, both of whom have very long memories and no hesitancy to make an example of those who cross them. That willingness to play hardball politics, and possessing the power to do so, is also a huge intangible that resides in Hillary's corner. Every political player considering supporting a candidate OTHER than Hillary has to calculate the risk of years of political purgatory for being on the losing side to the Clintons.

Many Democrats who would seem to have great appeal to voters in a general election have come to the conclusion that they simply cannot win the Democratic Party nomination either because of the powerful Clinton Machine or the sharp leftward tilts the Party apparatus, convention delegates and base have taken under the stewardship of DNC Chairman Howard Dean, and his acolytes within MoveOn.org and other far left political organizations.

Former Virginia Governor Mark Warner, for example, was poised to enter the race at one point but came to the conclusion that the delegates guaranteed to various interest groups, including labor unions, and minority groups, combined with the Super Delegates, made it virtually impossible to make the numbers work out for winning the nomination. If a guy who has many of the same characteristics as Bill Clinton (a politically moderate, successful, charismatic, Southern, Governor) cannot see a way to make the process work, how will the Democrats find candidates that fit any mold other than "extreme liberal" in the future?

With a clear understanding of the political terrain, the Clinton camp was able to map out and build an organization during the congressional cycle of 2006, while Clinton was running for re-election in New York. The Clintonistas were able to do this, largely with little consideration of the rest of the field. The Clintons were openly dismissive of Sen. John Kerry's toe-dipping for a second go at the nomination. John Edwards was viewed warily as a potential threat to a Clinton sweep through the South. Meanwhile the Clinton competitors were wary of the "Clintonistas" well-documented willingness to use their "weapons of personal destruction" to punish those who cross them.

The only wildcard in a Clinton coronation was first-term Illinois Senator Barack Obama, who was dubbed a rising star after his *tour-de-force* performance at the 2004 Democrat

National Convention, and his rock star status on the party's fundraising trail leading into the 2006 congressional election cycle. Obama's run is highlighted by an overly romanticized life story and an ability to connect with audiences' hearts and pocketbooks. Indeed, in the 2007 first quarter reporting period for presidential fundraising, Obama matched Clinton dollar for dollar in the race for donation dominance.

All that said, however, Obama's campaign is viewed as test run, albeit a serious one that must be respected and dealt with. With a light resume that requires more political seasoning, however, the consensus among the more senior strategists with Team Clinton is that the Obama bubble will burst.

Ultimately, Hillary has always been a disciplined and ambitious plodder. Like the tortoise and the hare, Obama will prove the flashier candidate, but Hillary has the staying power and holds all the important cards:[2]

- The money, organization and political connections.
- The unlimited will to do whatever it takes to win.

Republicans *may* select a consensus nominee who can unify the party and prevent a Hillary victory. However, each of the current top-tier Republican candidates has baggage which causes concern among critical constituencies in the party. In fact recent polls show that nearly six in ten Republican voters are dissatisfied with the current crop of choices.[3]

REPUBLICANS?

If current Republican front runner and former New York City Mayor Rudy Guiliani secures his party's nomination his pro-gay, pro-abortion, anti-gun track record and colorful

---

2   *There is one other potential Democratic candidate who could dramatically alter the equation: former Vice President Al Gore. Former President Bill Clinton referenced Gore as a potential candidate in an April 20, 2007 interview with Larry King.*

3   *NY Times/CBS News Poll, March 7-11, 2007, sampling 1,362 adults nationwide, including 698 Republicans.*

personal life could result in conservatives being less than engaged in the general election race. Worse, a Guiliani win could produce a third party candidacy backed by disgruntled conservatives that could result in a split vote similar to the one billionaire H. Ross Perot's candidacy created in 1992.[4] Bill Clinton won the White House with only 43% of the vote thanks to that split. Hillary is one of the most divisive figures in American politics, and she may not be able to convince more than half the country's voters to vote for her. But she can almost certainly get to 43%.

The Bush-Cheney team won re-election in 2004 over the Democrat ticket of Kerry-Edwards by about a three million vote margin, 50.7% to 48.3%.[5] The Electoral College vote was 286-251. With the current national climate, and without the powers of incumbency the Republicans possessed in 2004, Hillary should be able to improve on the Kerry-Edwards numbers. The bottom line is, that despite some current polling to the contrary, which shows Clinton with a better than 50% negative rating among likely voters, by the time November, 2008 rolls around she will likely be in position to beat any of the current Republican candidates in a head-to-head match up.

There are several reasons for this. First of all, Hillary will almost certainly have a huge gender advantage in 2008. Female voters have outnumbered males for the past three decades, with women accounting for 54% of the votes in the last presidential election.[6] In 2004, women voters outnumbered men at the ballot box by 8.4 million.[7] And, that gender gap in turnout will probably widen in 2008 with Hillary leading the ticket. A one

---

4 One potential third-party candidate if Giuliani gets the nomination may be Colorado Congressman Tom Tancredo, who has been a strong and vocal opponent to the Bush Administration's policies on illegal immigration. Tancredo recently named conservative commentator Bay Buchanan to head his presidential campaign organization. Buchanan is the sister of conservative commentator Pat Buchanan, and she ran all three of his presidential campaigns, including his run as the Reform Party candidate in 2000.

5 George W. Bush received 62,040,610 votes on Election Day 2004 to John Kerry's 59,028,439. www.uselectionatlas.org.

6 "2004 U.S. Presidential Election: National Election Poll," www.cnn.com/ELECTION/2004/pages/results/states/US/P/00/epolls.0.html.

7 Id.

point increase in turnout among women voters could mean a couple of million more votes for Hillary than what Kerry received.

But the gender advantage for Hillary is even bigger than those numbers reveal. The Gore-Lieberman ticket outpolled Bush 54-43% among women voters in 2000.[8] But Bush narrowed the gap with women considerably in 2004, losing that vote to Kerry by only 51-48%.[9] Hillary wins big if she merely regains the margin the Democrat ticket received in 2000.

The impact of swinging the gender gap becomes even more apparent when you look at *white* women voters. In fact, Bush's success in attracting a greater percentage of white women voters in 2004 than he did in 2000 was the key to his reelection.

In 2000 Bush edged Gore by only one point among white women (49-48%). However, Bush drilled Kerry by eleven points (55-44%) in 2004 among this critical demographic group. The five million additional votes that Bush picked up thanks to that shift among white women kept him in the White House.

Hillary will also be primed to increase the numbers that Kerry pulled in 2004 from African-American and Hispanic voters because of the popularity of her husband, Bill. And if Hillary selects Senator Barack Obama as her running mate he would provide additional appeal and excitement for black voters in particular.

In 2004, African Americans cast 12% of the total votes in the presidential race – 2% more than their share four years earlier. An increase of just one percentage point among black voters would increase the vote total for a Clinton-Obama ticket over that captured by Kerry in 2004 by about a million votes. That alone would trim the Bush margin of victory in 2004 by a

8   Id., 2000 U.S. Presidential Election results.
9   Id., 2004 U.S. Presidential Election results.

third! The Electoral College impact could be even more significant depending upon *where* those additional votes came from.

The charisma that Barack Obama would bring to the table is undeniable. Despite his relative inexperience on the national stage that factor would also enable him to bring a fresh, "new face" benefit to a potential Hillary-Obama ticket. Hillary could make the argument that her Administration would not simply be a rerun, or do-over, of the Bill Clinton Administration; with Obama on the team, it would be a blend of the "best" of the Clinton years with the promise of fresh ideas and new perspectives.

Or, Hillary might pick New Mexico Governor Bill Richardson as her running mate in a bid to appeal to the growing Hispanic voting base in the country. In 2000, the Gore team carried the Hispanic vote by 62%-35% over Bush. Kerry won the Hispanic vote again in 2004, but only by a 9% margin. Hispanics accounted for 8% of the total vote in 2004. Based on the growth patterns among Hispanics in America, that number will likely be 10% in 2008. If a Clinton-Richardson ticket got the same percentage of the vote Gore got in 2000, they would pull 2.3 million more Hispanic votes than Kerry did. If a Clinton-Richardson ticket increases the Hispanic share of the vote to 12% -- roughly equal to the African American share – the numbers improve dramatically for the Democrats.

The effect of having a Hispanic on the ticket has even larger Electoral College implications. Bill Richardson would almost certainly bring out enough votes in his home state to swing New Mexico's five electoral votes from the Republican column in 2004 to the Democrat column in 2008. (Bush only carried the state by a margin of 49.84% to Kerry's 49.05% in 2004; and Gore carried the state in 2000.) Richardson could also have an impact in Nevada, which Bush carried by only 50.47% to 47.88% over Kerry. That would swing another five electoral votes.

Iowa was in Gore's column in 2000, but shifted back to the Republicans in 2004 by a very slim margin, 49.90% to 49.23%. The Clinton-Richardson combo could slide Iowa back into the Democrat camp and move seven more Electoral College votes in the process.

Finally, what about Florida? No state provided more drama for the 2000 election than the Sunshine State, ultimately carried by Bush to the persistent chagrin of Al Gore. Would Richardson provide sufficient appeal to Florida's large Hispanic population and move that state's 27 electoral votes from the Republican column into the Democrat's column? Is so, we may all learn the Spanish term for "landslide victory" — *victoria aplastante*.

Can Republicans counter the voter appeal of the Clinton-Richardson (or Clinton-Obama) ticket with any combination of their current slate of candidates? Guiliani-McCain? Romney-Guiliani? McCain-Romney? The numbers just don't seem to add up for a Republican win.

Now, it can certainly be argued that male voters might not be excited about a Hillary candidacy and that whatever gains she may make among women voters will be offset among men. Bush won over Gore in 2000 by eleven points among male voters, 53-42%. (Ralph Nader got 3% of the male vote.) Bush improved on those numbers against Kerry, winning 55-41% in 2004.

However, the bulk of the male gender gap advantage enjoyed by Republicans in recent years can be traced directly to the overwhelming and consistent support of white men. Bush drubbed Gore 60-36% among white men in 2000, but saw only modest improvement over those numbers against Kerry in 2004, when Bush pulled a 62-37% win in that group. Theoretically, that gap could widen a bit more with a Hillary candidacy, but there is presumably a ceiling and it is not likely that any of the current crop of GOP candidates can expand the lead among white men enough to outpace her appeal to women voters.

There are also plenty of opportunities for the Republicans to make gains in the Electoral College in 2008. Kerry barely carried the states of New Hampshire (50.24% to 48.87%), Wisconsin (49.7% to 49.32%), Minnesota (51.09% to 47.61%) and Pennsylvania (50.92% to 48.42%) in 2004. Those states represent forty five critical electoral votes that could be shifted *if* the right candidate can overcome the gender and ethnic advantages that are consistently enjoyed by the Democrats. But who among the current crop of leading Republican Party contenders has the ability to swing any, much less all, of those states?

It is also important to consider the states that Bush narrowly carried over Kerry; states that will certainly be in play for the Democrats in 2008. Iowa, New Mexico, Ohio and Nevada were in the Republican column in 2004, two by a margin of less than one percent! Do any of the current Republican contenders bring any particular advantages to the race that can strengthen their party's hold on these states?

Hillary Rodham Clinton is seemingly poised to win the nation's highest office in 2008…unless Fred Dalton Thompson enters the race. In fact, the charismatic, Reaganesque Fred Dalton Thompson may be the *only* potential candidate who can prevent Hillary Rodham Clinton from being sworn into office at noon, January 20, 2009.

Perhaps more importantly, he may be one of the few national political figures who can heal the contentious Red-Blue split which has marked American politics in recent years. The numbers are shaping up for a big win for Hillary Clinton in 2008, but that is **before** the Fred Factor is added to the equation.

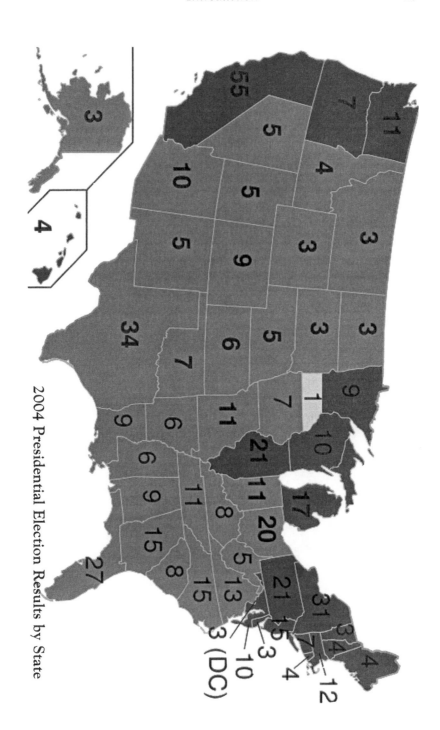

2004 Presidential Election Results by State

Section I:
Who is Fred Thompson?

CREATING HIS OWN DESTINY

Fred Thompson is a self-made man. He is one of those guys that might be described as the sort that "men want to be and women want to be with." He is a larger than life personification of the American dream. A living, breathing version of a "profile in courage."[10]

Fred Dalton Thompson was born on August 19, 1942 in tiny Sheffield, Alabama to Fletcher and Ruth Bradley Thompson. There was little in his early days that would have caused anyone to think he might someday be positioned to become President of the United States. Perhaps the only clue to what he would become may have been the fact that he spent his childhood and began his career in Lawrenceburg, Tennessee. Lawrenceburg was also the home of frontiersman and former Tennessee Congressman David Crockett.[11]

Lawrenceburg is blue-collar country in a red state. Manufacturing is king, with assembly lines churning out an array of goods from cheerleader uniforms to caskets. It sounds cliché, but Thompson climbed from those humble beginnings to become one of the most recognized faces – and voices — in the United States.

Fred's father sold used cars while his mother took care of the

---

10   "Profiles in Courage" was written by then-Senator John F. Kennedy and won a Pulitzer Prize in 1957. It details the bravery and integrity eight U.S. Senators who defied public opinion or crossed party lines to do what they believed was the right thing to do. All suffered public criticism and loss of popularity for their actions.

11   Crockett was always known as David; he is only known as Davy thanks to the Disney version of his life. He was actually born in Greene County, in East Tennessee, and his last home in the state was in Gibson County, in West Tennessee, but Lawrenceburg also claims him.

house. Neither of his parents graduated from high school, although his father did earn his high school equivalency certificate later in life. His family ate dinner every night at 6:00 P.M. "It was like clockwork," Thompson has said.[12] Like many rural Tennessee families at the time, life was anything but easy. "I grew up not having anything to live up to from an economic or professional standpoint, but having a lot to live up to from a growing-up and becoming-a-man standpoint," Thompson recalls.[13]

Thompson grew to man-sized proportions early, reaching his six-foot-five-inch frame early. He excelled in sports at Lawrence County High School – including football and basketball — but classmates remember him as the kind of kid who protected his fellow pupils from bullies.

Thompson's natural athletic skills did not extend to the classroom. At one point several of his teachers worked together to strip him of the title given to him by a vote of his peers — Most Athletic — because his grades were so poor. Some of those teachers would probably be surprised, but incredibly proud, at how things have turned out for the big kid who had such seemingly small ambitions.[14]

After graduating from high school in 1960 Thompson began working days in the local post office and nights as an assembly line worker at the Murray Ohio Bicycle plant so he could earn enough money to pay for college. At 17 he had married Sarah Elizabeth Lindsey, his high-school sweetheart, and for the first year of their marriage they lived first with her parents and then in public housing while scrimping and saving for college.[15]

---

12 Stephen F. Hayes, "From the Courthouse to the Whitehouse," Weekly Standard, April 23, 2007.
13 Id.
14 Retired General Tommy Franks tells the story of returning to a high school reunion in Midland, Texas after he became a General. His high school principal noted that he didn't remember Franks being "the brightest bulb in the socket." Franks responded: "Ain't this a great country." Fred Thompson would certainly agree.
15 Their first child, Tony, was born soon after they were married. Two more children, Daniel and Betsy, arrived while Fred was in law school.

He began his college studies at Florence State College in Florence, Alabama. (It is now the University of North Alabama.) Thompson attended Florence State for three semesters before he and Sarah enrolled together at Memphis State University (now known as the University of Memphis). Both of them worked hard to pay the bills and support their three young children. "I sold clothing, I sold shoes. I sold baby shoes. I sold ladies shoes. I worked in a factory," Thompson remembers.[16]

Sarah's uncle and grandfather were both lawyers. The desire to live up to the professional standards of her family proved to be a great motivator for the young man. Thompson got serious about his academics and successfully graduated from Memphis State with a double major in political science and philosophy in 1964. He was the first in the Thompson family to complete college. Thompson's new-found academic prowess also earned him scholarship offers from both Tulane and Vanderbilt University law schools.

He chose Vanderbilt. "We were probably the two guys least likely to succeed in our class," according to the late Howard Liebengood, who was a friend of Thompson's in law school.[17] Liebengood has said he and Thompson felt out of place at Vanderbilt because they graduated from state universities, while many of their peers attended prestigious private schools.[18] With three children and a wife, Thompson also did not have time for the campus rebellions and activism that dominated the Sixties.

---

16 Hayes, "From the Courthouse…," Weekly Standard.
17 "Could Lawyer-Actor-Senator Be VP?", USA Today, July 5, 2000. Liebengood would later serve both Fred Thompson and Bill Frist as Chief of Staff of their Senate offices. He passed away in January, 2005.
18 Id.

POLITICAL BEGINNINGS

U pon graduation from law school in 1967 the Thompson family headed back to Lawrenceburg where he began practicing law with his wife's uncle in the firm of Lindsey and Thompson. He also got involved in local politics.[19]

In 1969, he got his first big political break when he was appointed assistant U.S. attorney for the Middle District of Tennessee by Attorney General John Mitchell.[20] It was just the start of his active, and lifelong, involvement in politics.

In 1968, Thompson had served as the campaign manager for the losing Tennessee Seventh Congressional District campaign of John T. Williams. Two years later he worked on Chattanooga businessman Bill Brock's successful bid to unseat Senator Albert Gore, Sr.[21]

In 1972, at the urging of Lamar Alexander, Thompson resigned his position with the U.S. Attorney's Office to manage U.S. Senator Howard Baker's re-election campaign in Middle Tennessee.[22] Baker was successful in his re-election bid. The politically powerful triumvirate of Baker, Alexander and Thompson would intersect many times over the next four decades.

THE WATERGATE HEARINGS

S oon after the election was concluded Fred was called upon to assist Senator Baker as Minority Counsel for the Senate Select Committee on Presidential Campaign Activities (the Watergate Committee). He served in that capacity from

19 Thompson was already interested in national politics while in law school and showed his conservative bent early by backing Goldwater in the 1964 Presidential Election.
20 Mitchell was later among the Nixon Administration officials that Thompson questioned during the Watergate hearings.
21 Brock later served as Ronald Reagan's U.S. Trade Representative and Secretary of Labor.

1973-74. Part of his charge was to conduct an unbiased investigation into Watergate. He did that, even though it meant that his fellow Republicans – both those who were involved directly in Watergate and those who ran for office under the Republican banner in 1974 – would pay the price.[23]

Thompson ultimately played a significant role in the Watergate hearings. It was his investigation and line of questioning that revealed Nixon's extensive taping system. On July 16, 1973, Thompson asked Nixon aide Alexander Butterfield the question: "Mr. Butterfield, are you aware of the installation of any listening devices in the Oval Office of the president?"

The existence of these tape recordings were a surprising revelation to most of the country, but the line of questioning was not a surprise attack on an unsuspecting witness. In fact, this question had already been answered by Butterfield the previous Friday, during questioning by investigators of the minority and majority staffs. By Monday, the White House had been prepped for the story to come out because Thompson had phoned White House counsel Fred Buzhardt over the weekend to inform him that the Committee knew about the tapes.[24]

After some debate, it had been decided that Thompson would ask the key question during the televised hearings as a show of the Republicans' commitment to uncovering the truth.[25] Some of Thompson's Democrat critics who worked on the Watergate Committee say this was typical of Thompson and his showboating. Former Watergate investigator Scott Armstrong has said: "All of the investigating was done in

22 Coincidentally, his resignation came just one day before the Watergate burglary that would eventually take him to Washington for his first performance on a national stage.

23 In 1974 Alexander ran for Tennessee Governor and secured the Republican nomination but lost to Democrat Ray Blanton in the general election. Running as a Republican in 1974 was the "kiss of death" due to the fallout from the Watergate scandal. In fact, Blanton's campaign attacked Alexander for serving as an aide in the Nixon Administration. Four years later Alexander was elected to his first of two terms as Governor of Tennessee.

24 Michelle Cottle, "Another Beltway Bubba?", Washington Monthly, December, 1996.

25 Id.

private, then Thompson would try to set it up so that if there was a kill [during the hearings], he'd look like he was in on it."[26]

Some of his Democrat counterparts from the Watergate Committee see Thompson much differently. "Fred brings with him the grace of a Southern lawyer, and he's an excellent negotiator," says Sam Dash, Thompson's majority counterpart during the Watergate hearings. "He knows how to look laid back even when he's not. He can tell a joke and drawl his voice to make everybody feel he's not under anxiety. He'll get you talking about an entirely different topic, and then from out of nowhere comes the punch."[27]

Thompson is credited with feeding Baker the famous line that helped lead to the downfall of President Nixon: "What did the President know and when did he know it?"[28] He also pushed the Watergate Committee to investigate sacred cows such as the CIA, which was spending time and money investigating political enemies instead of America's enemies.[29]

BRINGING DOWN A GOVERNOR

Once the Watergate Committee completed its work Thompson returned home to Tennessee and set up a law practice with a couple of close friends and former law school classmates from Vanderbilt. The firm established offices in both Nashville and Washington, D.C.

In 1977, Thompson took up an against-all-odds case of a state government-official-turned-whistleblower who was viciously smeared after she sounded the alarm about a corrupt Tennessee governor.

---

26 Id.
27 Id.
28 Hayes, "From the Courthouse...," Weekly Standard.
29 Thompson detailed his Watergate Committee experiences in his book "At That Point In Time: The Inside Story of the Senate Watergate Committee," published in 1975 by Quadrangle.

Marie Ragghianti, a single mother of three children, was chairman of the Tennessee Pardons and Paroles Board. Over time she came to realize that the Governor was apparently trading the release of serious criminals for cash payments. On August 3, 1977, Governor Ray Blanton fired Ragghianti when she refused to release certain prisoners, who were later proved to have bribed members of the Blanton Administration for their release. Not content with simply dismissing her from her position, Blanton then set his media friends upon her, smearing Ragghianti's reputation.

Thompson, who had previously threatened legal action against the Blanton Administration on behalf of other state employees allegedly terminated for political reasons, was retained by Ragghianti.

Thompson filed a wrongful termination suit against the Governor which led to exposure of the "pardons and paroles" scandal. In July 1978, a jury found that Mr. Blanton had fired her "arbitrarily and capriciously," ordered that she be reinstated and awarded her $38,000 in back pay.

The "pardon and paroles" scandal picked up steam in late 1978 as Gov. Blanton, who had not sought re-election, was winding down his term in office. On December 14, the governor held a Christmas party where his staff presented him with a present: a metallic-blue Lincoln Continental.[30]

The next day, FBI agents swarmed into the Capitol in Nashville and seized hundreds of documents on pardons and clemency actions.[31] Soon thereafter, the FBI announced the arrest of the governor's legal counsel, T. Edward Sisk, and two others. A week later, the governor appeared before a federal

---

30 John Fund, "In 1978 Clinton Got A Close Look At The Dangers Of Selling Forgiveness," Jewish World Review, February 15, 2001.

31 One of the FBI agents who lead the investigation into the activities of Governor Ray Blanton, Hank Hillin, later detailed the story in his book "FBI Codename TENNPAR", Pine Hill Press (1985).

grand jury and declared his innocence. "I never took a dishonest dollar in my life."[32]

Pressure mounted for Gov. Blanton to be removed early and reached a fever pitch late on Jan. 15, 1979, after he finished a three-hour meeting with the announcement he had granted clemency to fifty two Tennessee inmates. His explanation to the media? He was under a court order to reduce overcrowding in the state prisons.[33]

The Governor was very selective, however, in how he reduced that overcrowding. One of the freed inmates, was Roger Humphreys, the son of a Blanton political crony. Humphreys was serving a 20- to 40-year sentence for murdering his former wife and her boyfriend. Despite the heinous nature of the crime, Humphreys had pumped 18 bullets from a two-shot Derringer into the couple, the corrupt Tennessee Governor called him "an outstanding, fine young man" and arranged for him to work outside the prison as a state photographer.

On January 15, he signed Mr. Humphrey's release papers in office with a rhetorical flourish: "This takes guts." At that point, his Secretary of State, Gentry Crowell, piped up: "Some people have more guts than brains."[34]

Crowell would later face his own share of political scandal as part of another FBI investigation. "Operation Rocky Top" became the FBI's code name for a public corruption investigation into the illegal sale of bingo licenses in the late 1980s which resulted in the eventual suicide of Crowell (by gunshot to the head) and the incarceration of several other political leaders, most notably Democrat State House Majority Leader Tommy Burnette.

The release of Humphreys produced an immediate outcry in

32 Id.
33 Id.
34 Id.

the state. On Jan. 17, three days before Gov. Blanton's term was to expire, U.S. Attorney Hal Hardin, a Democratic appointee, called Gov.-elect Lamar Alexander to tell him that Gov. Blanton was preparing papers to free as many as 18 more prisoners.

After a hurried series of meetings between Mr. Alexander and top legislative leaders, including advice from Fred Thompson, it was decided to quickly swear-in the new governor. The ceremony took place on live television in the offices of the state Supreme Court. Gov. Alexander told the state that he had agreed to be sworn in early because there was "substantial reason to believe" Gov. Blanton was preparing to release some targets of the grand jury investigation into the pardon scandal. The offices of Governor Blanton were even nailed shut to prevent the removal of evidence.[35]

Two Blanton aides were eventually convicted of selling pardons, while a third was acquitted. Blanton himself was later indicted and convicted for selling a liquor license in exchange for forgiveness of a $40,000 debt. He served two years in federal prison and died in 1996, still protesting his innocence.[36]

Democrat House Speaker Ned McWherter (who would succeed Lamar Alexander as Governor eight years later) and Democrat Lt. Governor John Wilder were completely cooperative in the early removal of Governor Ray Blanton from office. Wilder would later call it "impeachment Tennessee-style."

FROM TENNESSEE TO TINSELTOWN

The Ragghianti case attracted a lot of media attention, both within the State of Tennessee and far beyond. A book detailing Marie Ragghianti's bravery in bringing down a corrupt Governor was published in 1983 by Peter Maas

---

35 Id.
36 Id.

– who had also written *Serpico*. The book, *Marie: A True Story*, became a best seller.[37] Stories about underdogs who prevail against all the odds make for great books – and movies.

Film director Roger Donaldson bought the movie rights to Maas' book. Soon after purchasing the rights, Donaldson traveled to Nashville to meet with the real people involved in the story. When he met Thompson and saw the commanding presence and heard the gravely voice, Donaldson asked if he would like to portray himself in the movie. Fred agreed to play the role of "Fred Thompson"; many viewers of his later films would say that has never changed and that Thompson never really "acts" – he just plays "Fred Thompson."

Marie starred Sissy Spacek (who won an Oscar playing another Tennessean, Loretta Lynn, in *Coal Miner's Daughter*), Jeff Daniels and Morgan Freeman. The 1985 film also starred Fred Dalton Thompson in his first movie role.

While his movie and television career was just getting launched, Thompson's twenty five year marriage to Sarah was coming to an end. The couple divorced in 1985, the same year *Marie* premiered. The divorce was amicable, and the two have remained good friends over the years. In fact, she was an active supporter during his later campaigns for the U.S. Senate and remains willing to champion the Fred Thompson cause today. "That speaks to his character more than anything else," says Tom Ingram, a long-time Thompson advisor and friend. Ingram is, not coincidentally, a long-time advisor and current Chief of Staff to Tennessee Senator Lamar Alexander.

Marie was not a big hit at the box office, but when Donaldson needed someone to play the role of CIA director in his next film, *No Way Out* (with a young Kevin Costner in a starring role), he turned to Thompson. A string of movies followed, including: *The Hunt for Red October* (1990) with Sean Connery, *Days of Thunder* (1990) with Tom Cruise, *Die Hard 2*

---

37   Peter Maas, "Marie," Random House, (1983).

(1990)[38] with Bruce Willis, *Class Action* (1991), *Unnecessary Roughness* (1991), *Cape Fear* (1991), and *In the Line of Fire* (1993) with Clint Eastwood[39]. There were also cameo appearances on TV's *Matlock* during the same period.

Fred has often joked about his movie roles, once telling Sam Donaldson that whenever "they need an old, beat-up, middle-aged guy who'll work cheap, they call me."[40] A 1994 *New York Times* profile of Thompson described the authoritative character roles he has played as being an easy fit for him. "The glowering, hulking Mr. Thompson has played a White House chief of staff, a director of the Central Intelligence Agency, a highly placed F.B.I. agent, a rear admiral, even a senator. When Hollywood directors need someone who can personify governmental power, they often turn to him."[41]

Those who know him well say that the man on television is the same man you meet in real life. "He plays the person he really is," says Bob Davis, Thompson's former State Director and current Chairman of the Tennessee Republican Party. "He has always had leadership roles either on the big screen or in real life. He's not acting. That's him you see on the screen and America is thirsting for someone of his character to unite this country."

COAST TO COAST CAREER

Although his acting career was taking off, Thompson chose not to move to Hollywood but instead continued to live and work in Tennessee. He also spent time in Washington, D.C. with his legal and lobbying clients.

---

38 When Thompson starred with Cruise in Days of Thunder, he would tell people: "Cruise and I were crossing the street and all these ladies were just screamin' and hollerin'. Can you believe Cruise used to think they were screaming for him?"

39 There are also a few films that Thompson may hope people will forget, like Curly Sue (1990) and Baby's Day Out (1994).

40 December 25, 1994, ABC's This Week with Sam Donaldson.

41 Rick Bragg, "Grits and Glitter Campaign Helps Actor Who Played A Senator Become One," New York Times, November 12, 1994.

Thompson has always maintained that he was never really a lobbyist, merely "a lawyer who did some lobbying." Nevertheless, he represented some pretty high-powered clients during the 80s and 90s, including Westinghouse, General Electric, and the Teamsters pension fund.[42] The Memphis Commercial Appeal reported in 1994 that Thompson received a total of $507,000 in lobbying payments from 1975-1993.

Thompson was also actively involved in lobbying some pretty influential legislation. As representative for the Tennessee Savings and Loan League, Thompson lobbied for Senate passage of the Depository Institutions Amendments of 1982. Sponsored by former Sen. Jake Garn, this deregulation bill provided for additional government support of ailing S&Ls; increased the thrifts' freedom to invest in potentially more profitable, but riskier, ventures; and eliminated interest-rate ceilings on new accounts to increase S&Ls' competitiveness. This legislation has been blamed by some for laying the groundwork for the S&L collapse of the late '80s.[43]

Beginning in 1991, Thompson extended his representation and lobbying expertise to foreign entities. As an attorney with the Washington D.C. firm of Arent Fox Kitner Plotkin & Kahn, Thompson was registered as a foreign agent representing clients including a German mining group and Japan's Toyota Motor Corp.[44]

Critics of Thompson have claimed he also represented deposed Haitian President Jean–Bertrand Aristide. Thompson did file short form registration papers with the U.S. Justice Department to represent Haitian President Aristide in October 1991, two weeks after Aristide was overthrown. The filing lists Thompson as a member of the Washington-based law firm Arent Fox Kintner Plotkin & Kahn and says he intended to lobby Congress, the State Department and the White House "in order to obtain the restoration of the democratically elected

---

42 Cottle, *"Another Beltway Bubba," Washington Monthly.*
43 Id.
44 Id.

government of the Republic of Haiti."[45]

A Thompson spokesman has asserted that Thompson's representation actually involved the "Haitian embargo" and consisted of a single telephone call to then-White House Chief of Staff John Sununu.[46] Thompson was reportedly not paid for that contact and the representation was concluded at that time.

POLITICAL PATH

Thompson's career path took another dramatic turn in 1993 when Tennessee Senator Albert Gore, Jr. vacated his seat to assume his new position of Vice President of the United States. Ned McWherter, the Democrat Governor of Tennessee, appointed his chief deputy Harlan Mathews to fill the office until a special election could be held in November, 1994.[47]

From the outset it was understood that Mathews would simply be a caretaker in the Senate since he had no desire to run for the seat himself. Mathews had long been a loyal lieutenant to McWherter, who had been Speaker of the Tennessee House for 14 years before his election as Governor. The selection of Mathews enabled McWherter to reward a close friend for loyal service and also remain above the fray in the furious scramble to succeed Gore in the Senate. It also created an "open seat" scenario in Tennessee with both parties having ample opportunity to prepare for a fight.[48]

At the urging of Lamar Alexander and Howard Baker, Thompson decided to run for the U.S. Senate. He announced

---

45 Kenneth Vogel, "*Law and Order Lobbying,*" *www.politico.com, April 2, 2007.*
46 *Id.*
47 *Mathews spent 13 years as Tennessee's State Treasurer before being appointed as Deputy Governor in 1987. In Tennessee the State Treasurer is elected by vote of the General Assembly.*
48 *1994 would prove to be a big political year in Tennessee as the state's other Senator, Democrat Jim Sasser, faced reelection that year. McWherter was also term limited as Governor, setting up an open seat race for Governor that year as well.*

his candidacy from the Lawrenceburg town square on April 16, 1994.

The leading Democrat candidate for the seat was a young Tennessee Congressman named Jim Cooper, who had the strongest credentials of any non-incumbent in the country that year. Cooper was the son of a former Tennessee Governor. He was a Rhodes Scholar. He had graduated from Harvard Law School. At the age of 40 he already had 12 years in Congress under his belt and had amassed a fairly conservative voting record. He was recognized as a healthcare expert and had raised money for his campaign quickly and efficiently despite refusing to accept PAC donations. He was heavily favored to keep "the Gore seat" in Democrat hands.

Thompson had entered the race relatively late. By the time he formally kicked off the campaign in Lawrenceburg, Cooper was leading by a three-to-two margin in most polls and had raised three times as much money as Thompson.[49] Cooper's $2.5 million war chest was the largest of any non-incumbent in the country.

MULE DAY

If you're not from Tennessee, Mule Day is hard to explain. Actually, if you *are* from Tennessee Mule Day is hard to explain.

Mule Day takes place every April in Columbia, Tennessee – the self-proclaimed Mule capitol of the world. It has been a traditional local event since 1840.

Mule Day is a festival and parade and flea market all rolled into one. Visitors are treated to fast-paced bluegrass music and the smells of barbeque and homemade pies float through the air. In fact, it is such an institution with so many thousands of

---

49 *For example, a February, 1994 poll had Thompson trailing Cooper 36% to 17%.*

people flocking to it that the Department of Homeland Security has placed Mule Day on its list of possible terrorism targets.

And if you're running for office in Tennessee, you had better be at Mule Day.

No governor, no senator, no state representative – no one running for *dogcatcher* can skip Mule Day and expect to win office. Tennesseans come from miles around to meet candidates, shake their hands, look them in the eye and take their measure.

Matt King, a Tennessee Republican activist, remembers the pit in his stomach when he arrived at Mule Day in April, 1994 and saw Cooper there and actively campaigning while Fred Thompson was noticeably missing.

In fact, King watched Cooper work the Mule Day parade route in downtown Columbia, wearing a 'Vote for Cooper' t-shirt over his button-down shirt. He was going from person to person, shaking hands and greeting many of those along the parade route by name.

To be generous, Cooper appears more at home in a university classroom than he does at a down-home event such as Mule Day. King recalls seeing Cooper, "Short, with glasses, a bit mousey and talking health care to people about to see a parade of mules." But Cooper was starting to build a crowd around him.

"We're done for," King recalls thinking. "It's the biggest event of the year. You've got to go to Mule Day. Where is Fred?!?!"

Then King heard a cheer coming up from behind him.

In the parade, looking like a giant amidst the mules and parade floats was a tall man on a dark horse waving at the crowd. He was smiling, wearing blue jeans, flannel shirt and a cowboy hat.

King squinted. Then he cheered. The man on the horse was Fred Thompson.

The noisy clip-clop of the horse overtook the wonkish policy speech that Cooper was giving to the folks gathered on the sidelines. When they got close to Cooper, Fred took off his hat, waved it at the crowd and pulled up on the reins just a bit. The large horse with the even bigger guy on its back drew back, whinnied and Fred flashed a hero's smile. It wasn't quite the two back legs rear that the Lone Ranger made fashionable, but it was close enough for Mule Day.

Those people listening to Cooper left him immediately – they were all drawn to Fred in the parade, King remembers. Unfortunately for Thompson, the Mule Day campaign style and success was the exception rather than the rule during the early months of his campaign for the U.S. Senate.

THE CAMPAIGN STALLS

In the August primary, Thompson dispatched fellow Republican John Baker, a Memphis salesman, to win the nomination. But despite the fact that Baker was unknown and severely under-funded, Thompson received little over three-fifths of the Republican primary vote. Thompson's star power and campaign work ethic were being questioned aloud by Republicans and Democrats alike.

Long after the campaign was over, Thompson still bristled easily from the criticism he received during the campaign: "It seems like the experts are always fighting the last war and really don't have the ability to project - here in Tennessee especially. The way they saw it, Cooper had a million dollars going in, was the fair-haired boy of the health care industry, and was an effective campaigner. The fact of the matter was the only race he'd ever had was that first race for Congress 12 years ago."[50]

While Cooper had only run one tough campaign, he had run it successfully and against some of the same powerful Republican machinery that was being brought against him in 1994. Running in a newly-created, swing district that sprawled 300 miles across the rural interior of the state, Cooper faced Cissy Baker, whose father was Thompson mentor Howard Baker. Baker spent a then-record $1.2 million, but Cooper crushed her by a two to one margin.[51]

Thompson's campaign manager, Bill Lacy, would later explain that the initial low profile of the campaign was planned. "We knew little attention was going to be paid to our race during the primary season, with a big, well-financed field shaping up in the Republican primary for the other seat," Lacy later recounted. "So we concentrated on raising money for the big media push that would start the day after the primary in mid-August."[52]

That plan certainly made some sense as the Republican Primary battle for the opportunity to unseat Democrat incumbent Senator Jim Sasser had attracted a large field of candidates. A young physician from Nashville named Bill Frist ended up winning that very expensive primary. In one of the biggest political upsets in the nation in 1994, Frist went on to unseat Sasser in November. Just eight years later, Frist was elected Majority Leader of the U.S. Senate.[53]

The Thompson campaign team was certainly experienced enough to overcome the long odds they seemed to face. Lacy was Tennessee native and a veteran Republican political

50 David Bieler, *"The Senator From Central Casting, Campaigns and Elections*, May 1, 1995.
51 Id.
52 Id.
53 One of the other Republican candidates in that primary race, Bob Corker, was elected in 2006 to succeed Senator Frist. Frist had promised not to seek more than two terms when he was first elected.

operative. He had managed Bob Dole's 1988 bid for the Presidency and had assembled a top flight campaign team for Thompson that included pollster Linda DiVall and media expert Alex Castellanos.

During the Primary, the Thompson campaign ran only one television spot. The commercial was a biographical introduction that shared some of his various adventures as a prosecutor, Watergate investigator, crusader against corruption in the Governor's office and actor. It was intended to help voters make the connection between the face they recognized from the movies and the man running for the U.S. Senate.[54] It took a while for voters to make that link, and until they did, it looked as though Thompson might not only lose, but lose badly.

Longtime Tennessee political journalist and activist Frank Cagle recalls one particularly hot summer day in 1993 when Thompson was just beginning to travel the state. He arrived at a political event in Sevier County, the Republican-dominated eastern part of the state, where Cagle and a few of his friends were waiting outside a big tent where the event was to take place. "We looked over the fairgrounds to see a tall fellow we recognized from the movies wandering around like he was lost. He evidently didn't get the memo about it being a casual event. He had left his suit coat and tie in the car and had rolled up the sleeves of his white shirt. He wandered up, sweating like a pig."[55]

It was Thompson's first campaign appearance in that part of the state, and the consensus from Cagle and his buddies after talking to him was that Cooper would eat him alive. Watching Thompson campaign at other events over the next year left Cagle with the sense that he just wasn't comfortable with the glad-handing "grip and grin" approach. "His speeches were OK, but not spellbinding. They tended to be a little too abstract, too much from his background as a Senate staffer, a federal

---

54   Id.
55   Frank Cagle, "Meet Fred," Metro Pulse, May 2, 2007.
56   Id.

prosecutor and an attorney. But he got better as he went along. His problem was his attitude. He generally looked miserable and had the air of a man who wondered why he was there."[56]

Thompson himself began to question what he was doing and how he was doing it. At a low point in the campaign, Thompson met at a Cracker Barrel restaurant with Tom Ingram to talk about the race. He told the long time political strategist and friend that he wasn't having any fun campaigning and was pessimistic about his prospects against Cooper. In fact, Thompson confided that he was thinking about dropping out of the race. "Fred was beleaguered by the traditional way of running for office," Ingram remembers. "He was expressing his misery over things."[57]

Ingram asked Thompson a question: "What would you do if you ran the way you wanted to run?" Thompson thought for a minute, then said he "would go to his Dad's used car lot (in Lawrenceburg), get a pick-up truck and drive across the state." Ingram said, "Do it."[58]

Fred decided to follow his instincts and get a truck. "People thought he was crazy", Ingram recalls. "It worked because it wasn't an unnatural or unreal thing for him to do."

THE BIG RED TRUCK

The next decision centered on the exact kind of truck Fred should drive around the state. "Red made sense," according to Ingram. "We didn't want anything too flashy, so "used" made sense. We wanted something that was going to be roomy because there were going to be people with him from time to time, so we got a stretch cab."[59]

---

57 Hayes, "From the Courthouse..." *Weekly Standard.*
58 Gail Kerr, "Will Fred's Old, Red Pickup Ride Again On Presidential Trail?" *Tennessean,* March 18, 2007.
59 Id.

On August 5, 1994, the 1990 cherry-red, extended cab Chevy pickup truck with four on the floor and almost 213,000 miles on it hit the campaign trail with Fred Thompson in the front passenger seat.[60] The campaign leased it for $500 a month. The big red truck soon achieved a personality of its own, and it was even featured on campaign buttons. At campaign stops people clamored to have their pictures taken with Fred... and the truck.

The Cooper campaign complained that the truck was just a Hollywood-style gimmick designed to make Thompson look down to earth. "But if the truck had not been authentic it would have been about as successful as Michael Dukakis in a tank—the photo op that came to symbolize a losing 1988 presidential campaign," Frank Cagle points out. "Fred fit in the truck. Dukakis didn't fit in the tank."[61]

"[The truck] was more than a device," Ingram maintains. "It made Fred comfortable as a candidate. He felt liberated to just be himself."[62]

This was not the first time that Ingram was part of developing a so-called gimmick in order to help a candidate better connect with the voters. In 1974, young lawyer Lamar Alexander lost a bid for Tennessee Governor in large part due to fallout from the Watergate Scandal. The fact that Alexander had been a White House aide in the Nixon Administration only served to exacerbate the effects of the scandal in his race. But he was also ill-served by campaigning across Tennessee in dark suits. "I flew around in a blue suit from one Rotary meeting to the next, preaching to the converted," Alexander recalls.

In 1978, Alexander again sought the Governor's office, but this time he was clad in a red-and-black plaid shirt and campaigned by walking across the entire state in order to personally connect with the voters. The campaign manager of

---

60   Id.
61   Cagle, "Meet Fred," Metro Pulse.
62   Hayes, "From the Courthouse..." Weekly Standard.

that race, who became Governor Alexander's Chief of Staff and who now serves as his Senate Chief of Staff, was Tom Ingram. Alexander won handily in 1978 and by an even larger margin when he sought reelection four years later.

In 2006, Republican Senate nominee Bob Corker was having a difficult race against the charismatic and well-funded Democrat nominee Harold Ford, Jr. Tom Ingram was called in during the final months of the campaign to save the day. Ingram, described by Newsweek magazine as "rumpled, martini-drinking, cigar chewing veteran of Tennessee politics," again worked his magic and Corker prevailed.[63]

For the Thompson campaign, the big red truck had an immediate and positive impact on the race. "Cooper had Thompson by the gonads," recalls Bruce Dobie, who was editor of the alternative weekly newspaper the *Nashville Scene* at the time of the campaign.[64] The Cooper campaign was clicking on all cylinders while Thompson was struggling. "Suddenly, Thompson decides things aren't going right," Dobie recounts. "He decides he just wants to drive around the state and talk to people. There's a huge overthrow in the campaign, and the highly natural, organic, earthy farmer Fred Thompson is born. Soon, Cooper was so far behind he couldn't see straight."[65]

The revised campaign imagery of the Thompson campaign did not stop with the big red truck. Blue jeans and a flannel shirt became the campaign outfit of choice.[66]

For such imagery to be successful, however, the underlying authenticity must be there. Ingram notes that when Alexander walked across the state, it let him get closer to who he actually was, and it was that reality that resonated with Tennesseans

63 Richard Wolffe, "A GOP Balancing Act," *Newsweek*, October 30, 2006.
64 Cottle, "Another Beltway Bubba?" *Washington Monthly*.
65 Id.
66 *The campaign makeover continued in 1996 when Fred sought reelection to a full six year term. Fred's mother Ruth was featured in a television commercial where he promised not to touch Social Security. His campaign website even gave people the opportunity to download Mom's "Famous Fresh Coconut Cake and Coconut Cream Pie Recipes."*

much better than a guy in a blue suit. Likewise, the shift in campaign strategy for Thompson put him back in contact with his blue-collar roots and made him more comfortable with the voters. "It has to be real," Ingram says, "or it won't work."

Ron Ramsey, now Lieutenant Governor of Tennessee, was early in his own political career when he saw how Thompson turned that 1994 race around. "I know that are those that will say the red pickup was a prop, but it was always clear to me that he was more comfortable in that than in a suit," Ramsey said. "Every time I saw him you could tell he was in his element because he was so down to earth."

TURNING THE TIDE

There was a lot more to the 1994 Thompson campaign than simply a big red truck. He stood in the bed of that truck and railed against Big Government. "America's government is bringing America down, and the only thing that can change that is a return to the basics," he said on the stump. "We will get back to basics and make the sacrifices and once again amaze the world at how, in America, ordinary people can do very extraordinary things."[67] Thompson emphasized issues that would appeal to disaffected voters — making laws apply to the members of Congress who pass them; congressional pay raises; entitlement reform. The same issues contained in Newt Gingrich's "Contract With America" that carried Republicans to victory in the House provided a winning surge for Fred Thompson.

First the race tightened. Then Fred moved ahead and Cooper became more desperate in his attacks, even blasting Thompson as "a Gucci-wearing, Lincoln-driving, Perrier-drinking, Grey Poupon-spreading millionaire Washington special interest lobbyist." In one notable campaign exchange, Cooper claimed that Thompson had a secret life as a "foreign agent." Thompson cleverly retorted that Cooper had seen "too

67   Hayes, "From the Courthouse...", Weekly Standard.

many of my movies if he thinks I'm some sort of a secret agent."

Once he got out of the suits and in touch with his "inner good ol' boy", Thompson proved to be a campaigner. Richard Land, president of the Southern Baptist Convention's Religious and Ethics Liberty Commission, recently described Thompson as a "masterful retail politician." "Fred Thompson reminds me of a Southern-fried Reagan," Land said. "To see Fred work a crowd must be what it was like to watch Rembrandt paint."[68]

Tom Ingram, though, summed up Fred's campaign prowess up best: "When he's doing something he wants to do, nobody's got more energy, nobody's better at it."

Thompson won 61 percent of the vote, Cooper just 39 percent. Thompson was certainly helped toward victory by the historic Republican tide of 1994. But Cooper himself would later acknowledge that he had underestimated the power of Thompson's film career. "He was in so many movies," Cooper told the Nashville *Tennessean* in 2002. "I should have been more worried than I was because that is a powerful way to present yourself to the public."

The importance of his acting experience was also cited by Thompson as a big factor in his 1994 success. A November 1994 article in the Memphis *Commercial Appeal*, quoted Thompson saying he'd known all along that TV would be the driving force in the campaign: "The camera doesn't lie. It looks straight into your soul. I'm the only one in this race who has known it."[69] Thompson's skills have only improved over time.

And what happened to the big red truck? Thompson purchased it for $5000 and drove it to Washington for his first day of work. Today it sits in the driveway of his mother's house in Franklin, Tennessee with expired U.S. Senate tags and 300,000 miles on the odometer.[70]

68   Sam Youngman, "Evangelical Leader Warms to a Run By Thompson In '08", *The Hill*,
      April 4, 2007.
69   Cottle, "Another Beltway Bubba?" *Washington Monthly*.
70   Kerr, "Will Fred's Old Pickup…", *Tennessean*.

THE SENATE'S LEADING MAN

Because Fred Thompson won a special election for the seat vacated by Vice President Al Gore before the end of his term, he did not have to wait until the new Senators and Congressmen swept into office by the Republican high tide in November took office in January.[71] He was officially sworn in as a United States Senator by Senator Robert Byrd of West Virginia in the Senate Chamber on December 9, 1994. Fred not only got a bit of a bump in seniority, but he also got a head start on the job.

After being in office for less than a week, Thompson was tapped by Republican Senate Leader Bob Dole to give the Republican response to President Bill Clinton's "Middle-Class Tax Cut" address on December 15, 1994. The President's speech and Thompson's response were televised nationally. A photo caption in the next day's Washington Post read: "Sen. Fred Thompson: His charismatic delivery of the GOP response was reminiscent of Ronald Reagan."

In his plain spoken response to Clinton's announcement of a new tax plan, Thompson suggested that the President's sudden support for tax relief might be a product of "public opinion polls rather than real conviction." "Until a few weeks ago," Mr. Thompson said slowly, "they were even saying we didn't even need a tax cut. But from what I heard tonight, the President's vision for the future looks a lot like what Republicans just campaigned for, at least until we start looking at the details."[72]

The Clinton Administration expressed surprise at the choice the Republicans made in picking Thompson to deliver the response and grudging respect for the job that he did. White House strategist Paul Begala noted that he was hoping they

---

71 *In 1994 Republicans took majority control of both the House and Senate for the first time in 40 years.*

72 *Douglas Jehl, "GOP Picks New Senator To Respond To President," New York Times, December 16, 1994.*

would have "put [Bob] Dole or Newt [Gingrich] out there" instead of Fred.[73]

"Those of us who just came to town don't claim to have all the answers," Senator Thompson said in his remarks, which were broadcast live on all four major networks following the President's address. "I'm still unpacking my boxes. But one thing we do know. We know why you sent us here: to cut big government down to size, to turn Congress around and to set our country in a new direction. We campaigned on these principles, and now we're going to do something that has become all too unusual in American politics: we're going to do exactly what we said."[74]

Frank Rich of the *New York Times* was practically effusive in his praise of Thompson the following week: "Sitting casually on a desk and speaking a scant five minutes, the nation's newest Senator, Fred Thompson of Tennessee, delivered a G.O.P. rebuttal that had all the focus, intimacy and conviction that Mr. Clinton's impersonation of a Republican lacked."[75]

A few days later ABC's Sam Donaldson was pushing Thompson to comment on reports that Republicans were touting him as a potential challenger to President Clinton in the 1996 election. Thompson demurred. "There's one thing, I think, for certain that I've observed around here over the period of time that I've been here, and watching all this for years, and that is when people come to town, somewhere along the line, if they do anything at all, if they're shown to be able to put one foot in front of the other, they're mentioned for the national ticket. So now you've mentioned me, and I appreciate it, so we can move on to more serious topics."[76]

---

73 Id.
74 Id.
75 Frank Rich, "A Star Is Born," *New York Times*, December 22, 1994.
76 December 25, 1994, ABC's *This Week with Sam Donaldson*.

FIGHTING FOR THE TRUTH

Despite the high-profile start to his Senate career, some of Thompson's most effective work in the Senate was actually done outside the view of the spotlight, at least initially. Throughout his career Fred Thompson has been willing to take the side of the underdog, even when it meant taking on powerful interests arrayed against him. The Marie Ragghianti story was characteristic of Thompson's doggedness. The Lance Fielder story is yet another example of his refusal to back down when pursuing of truth and justice on behalf of others.

The story had its origins long before Thompson was a U.S. Senator and far from the valleys and mountains of Tennessee. In fact, it began 8,000 miles away, amidst whizzing bullets and hot-white tracers from a machine gun on a smoke-filled Iraqi desert during the first Gulf War. On an unused Iraqi airfield in a stretch of endless sand a politically connected and "medal hungry" Lt. Colonel buried the truth about the death of a young soldier from Nashville, Tennessee: Cpl. Douglas Lance Fielder. Without Fred Thompson's courage and his resolve to get results – aided by a father's grief – that truth, and a Pentagon cover-up, would have remained buried.

Lt. Colonel John H. Daly broke his own cease-fire order on that cold, black desert night of Feb. 27, 1991. Daly left 100 vehicles that were under his command behind as he led a charge forward and ordered the soldiers in his vehicle to open fire on what he said was the enemy. But there was no enemy in the desert that night.

The five U.S. soldiers stranded in Iraqi desert thought they were being rescued. Standing guard beside their broken-down ammunition carrier near the Iraqi town of Umm Hajul, the detachment of engineers from the Army's 1st Armored Division watched columns of M1A1 tanks and Bradley Fighting Vehicles approach from the north. One of the soldiers, Spc. Craig Walker, signaled the approaching vehicles by switching the infrared light on his night-vision goggles on and off. Help, he thought, was on the way.

Tragically, it was not. Troops from the 3rd Armored Cavalry Regiment, led by Daly, had mistakenly crossed into a sector occupied by other U.S. forces. They believed, however, that they were in enemy territory. Seeing the vehicle, Daly decided to attack the "enemy."

They opened fire on the five engineers. Taking cover in sand dunes behind their vehicles, the soldiers frantically radioed headquarters that they were taking friendly fire—but the firing continued. After seven deadly minutes, one of the engineers was wounded. Another, Cpl. Lance Fielder, lay dead from the bullets of an American machine gun.[77]

Instead of facing the consequences, Lt. Colonel Daly used his political connections to cover up the truth. He invented a story about how he thwarted an ambush by the Iraqi Republican Guard.

Why would Lt. Colonel Daly lie? Captain Bo Friesen believes he knows. He saw what happened that deadly night and the events sickened him. "The only way to get a medal for valor is to actually take part in the fighting," Friesen said. "Since there was very little fighting at hand, Daly could only win a decoration by personally charging forward."

Daly would have gotten away with it if not for Fred Thompson. This was no simple investigation. Anyone taking up Fielder's cause would need a platoon's worth of courage to get results. This was not just a U.S. Senator taking on a Lt. Colonel. This was a U.S. Senator taking on a Lt. Colonel who was backed by the Pentagon's military establishment – as powerful a force as any in Washington. In addition to that, Lt. Colonel Daly had acquired many friends in the nation's capital.

---

77 *Fielder was one of 35 Americans killed by "friendly fire" in the 1991 Persian Gulf War. That represents 24% of total 148 battle deaths in that war, the highest percentage for any U.S. military conflict in the 20th century.*

He had also married into the family of World War II hero and former Army Chief of Staff Creighton Abrams, the Abrams family moved in the Capitol's most powerful political circles.

By the time Fred Thompson began his quest for the truth, the Army brass had already conducted two investigations into the attack that killed Fielder. Those investigations were, in reality, little more than whitewashes.[78]

For example, one fellow officer filed a statement that directly led to Daly's Bronze Star:

> "[Daly's] valor was clearly demonstrated on the evening of 26 Feb and morning of 27 Feb when he participated in the assault of an enemy airfield... LTC Daly demonstrated outstanding leadership as he calmly and systematically orchestrated actions on the objective. We continued to encroach on the enemy position until within about 50 meters. LTC Daly dismounted part of his crew to begin clearing the objective while I maneuvered to the rear of the position to prevent the enemy's egress/assist in clearing the objective... During the entire ground war, but most specifically during the aforementioned night attack, LTC Daly's actions were both valorous and meritorious. He clearly demonstrated his ability to lead and to fight."

Soldiers who were there called that statement "a bold-faced lie." In truth, there was no enemy in the area that night. No gunfire was aimed or directed at Daly and his crew. There was only Cpl. Lance Fielder, his team and their Humvee which had broken down in the desert.

"We were originally told by the Army that he was killed by the Iraqi Republican Guard," said Ron Fielder, Lance's father. "It was several months later, when some of his friends who were with him got back, that we were told he was not killed by Iraqis.

---

78 A copy of the GAO (General Accounting Office) report dated April 7, 1995 can be found at www.fas.org/irp/gao/osi95010.htm.

He was killed by Americans. For over three years we could not find out anything about it."

Unable to get through the protective barrier that the Pentagon placed around Daly, Ron Fielder solicited the help of his U.S. Senator Fred Thompson. Armed with a report from the General Accounting Office – the watchdog arm of Congress –Thompson began hearings into the case.

"Lieutenant Colonel Daly conducted himself in a totally inappropriate way," Thompson said as he started this particular fight for justice. "He had 100 vehicles under his command and yet he took it upon himself to rush forward and let his gunner get into the action. I don't know whether somebody saw a *Patton* movie one too many times or what."

The investigation that Fred Thompson initiated revealed:

• Lt. Colonel Daly appeared to be in a rush to "get in some shots."

• Officers in Daly's command "were really medal hungry hounds" who kept asking: "When are we going to get to shoot something? When are we going to get to kill somebody?"

• Daly did not tell anyone there were friendly forces in the area.

• It was Daly who broke his own unit's cease-fire order and gave the go-ahead for his gunner to fire the shots that killed Fielder.

• When the truth began to seep out the Army reprimanded Daly, but the reprimand was never placed in Daly's personnel file. In fact, when Thompson began his inquiry, Daly was on the short list for a promotion to full Colonel.

- Cpl. Lance Fielder was shot though the leg in the first round of friendly fire. Despite the wound, he got a fellow engineer to safety, and warned the others in his team to dig in, in order to create better defensive positions. It was at that point that fire pounded the men, ripping through Fielder's chest.

"They were hiding it from us because the man responsible was a very high-ranking officer and had political connections," Ron Fielder said. "Fred spent about a year and a half working on this very hard. He didn't know me from Adam, but he never stopped working at it. He did a lot of hard work that he didn't have to do."

Thompson got results. Daly and others responsible for the "friendly fire" death of Fielder and the subsequent cover-up left the Army. On April 19, 1995, Army Secretary Togo West announced that three soldiers who had received heroism awards based upon "misleading" statements of the commanding officers had been stripped of their awards.[79]

Daly had political connections in both parties and had won his so-called "honors" under a Republican administration. But Thompson only cared that the truth was revealed, and he didn't mind taking on the military establishment and a Republican Administration to do it.

The medals distributed in connection with the incident by the officers who were responsible for the deadly friendly fire episode was of particular concern to Thompson. ``You can't look at that without asking yourself a question of whether the whole thing was used to reinvent the facts of that night to bail everybody out," Thompson said.

"I've not been around a lot of politicians," Ron Fielder said of Fred Thompson, "but after being around him I wish we had several hundred just like him." Fielder's son Lance was

---

79 *Associated Press, April 20, 1995.*

posthumously promoted to Sergeant and awarded a Bronze Star with a "V" for valor.

Despite the efforts of Fred Thompson to get to the truth in the Fielder "friendly fire" case, it appears that a culture of "cover-up" persists in such incidents. On April 22, 2004, former NFL football star Pat Tillman, who had left the stardom of pro football to enlist in the U.S. Army following 9-11, was killed in action in Afghanistan. Initially, the Pentagon claimed he had been killed when Tillman and his unit were attacked in an apparent ambush on a road outside of the village. An Afghan militia soldier was killed and two other Rangers were injured as well. Soon, however, it became apparent that Tillman had been killed by "friendly fire" and that the story of an "epic gunfight" were simply part of an intentional cover-up of the truth.[80]

ANOTHER SCANDAL INVESTIGATION

Despite receiving some encouragement to pursue the White House in 1996, Thompson sought a full six year term in the U.S. Senate.[81] West Tennessee criminal defense lawyer Houston Gordon was the Democrat's choice to challenge Thompson. It did not prove to be much of a challenge as Thompson won by a 61% to 39% margin. Additionally, Thompson received more votes than any candidate in Tennessee history.

Shortly after Thompson returned to Washington in January, 1997 to begin his first full term as a U.S. Senator, he would again take center stage in investigating another political scandal. As the new Chairman of the Senate's Committee on Governmental Affairs, he would oversee investigations into allegations that the government of the People's Republic of China (PRC) attempted to illegally influence American

---

80 Steve Coll, "Barrage of Bullets Drowned Out Cries of Comrades," Washington Post, December 5, 2004.

81 Thompson did, however, assist Republican Presidential nominee Bob Dole in preparing for his debates with Bill Clinton. Thompson stood in for Clinton in the mock debates.

politics prior to the 1996 elections.[82] There were also indications that the PRC had become involved in the fundraising activities of the Clinton White House as well.[83]

Questions about the Democratic National Committee's (DNC) fundraising efforts from foreign sources were first raised after a news report in the *Los Angeles Times* revealed that a $250,000 donation to the party from subsidiary of a South Korean electronics company had been refunded because it violated a ban on donations from foreign nationals in U.S. elections.[84] The DNC had issued a press release announcing the return of the funds. The Clinton Administration was implicated because John H.K. Lee, chairman of both the parent and subsidiary company, had attended an April, 1996 fundraiser where he met President Clinton.

Later, the PRC became embroiled in the controversy when the *Washington Post* reported that Justice Department investigators had learned that agents of the PRC had sought and coordinated contributions from foreign sources to the Democratic National Committee prior to the 1996 presidential campaign.[85]

According to the 9,600 page Final Report of the Governmental Affairs Committee, the PRC had become increasingly concerned about improving its image with the American people and its ability to influence the U.S. government as the business and trade interests of the two

82   Two books provide excellent factual background on the attempts of the PRC to influence the 1996 U.S. election cycle. Bill Gertz, The China Threat: How the People's Republic Targets America, Regnery (2002); Ed Timperlake and William Triplett, Year of the Rat, Regnery (1998).

83   The Final Report of the Committee on Governmental Affairs in connection with the "Investigation of Illegal or Improper Activities in Connection With 1996 Federal Election Campaigns" was issued March 10, 1998. www.fas.org/irp/congress/1998_rpt/sgo-sir/index.html

84   Alan C. Miller, "Democrats Return Illegal Contribution," LA Times, September 21, 1996.

85   Bob Woodward and Brian Duffy, "Chinese Embassy Role in Contributions Probed," Washington Post, February 13, 1997.

86   For example, total trade between the two countries had risen from $4.8 billion in 1980 to $63.5 billion in 1996, making China the fourth largest U.S. trading partner at the time.

countries were rapidly expanding.[86] The cozy relationship between the U.S. and Taiwan also concerned the PRC, particularly the fact that Taiwanese business interests seemed to have an advantage over those from the PRC.[87]

The election of a Republican-controlled House in 1994 intensified the concern of the PRC over its relationship with the U.S. because of their belief that the Republicans would be less friendly to Chinese interests. The Thompson Committee determined that the Clinton Administration's acquiescence to various congressional resolutions during that time period led the PRC to conclude that the influence of Congress over foreign policy was more significant than it had previously thought.[88]

The PRC vehemently denied that it ever extended its efforts in the U.S. beyond lobbying and into political contributions. "Recently, some people and media in the United States speculated again about so-called participation by Chinese individuals in political donations during the U.S. elections," a Chinese Foreign Ministry spokesman Zhu Bangzao said at a news briefing on May 20, 1998. "It is sheer fabrication and is intended to slander China. Beijing has never, nor will we ever, use money to influence American politics."[89] The complicated money trail told quite a different story.

Ultimately, twenty-two people were convicted for fraud or funneling illegal funds into the 1996 U.S. election process.[90] A number of the convictions came against longtime Clinton-Gore friends and political appointees, including longtime Clinton friend Charlie Trie, Clinton fundraiser Johnny Chung, DNC fundraisers John Huang and James Riady, and Maria Hsia (who hosted the infamous "Buddhist Temple" fundraiser for then-Vice President Al Gore).[91]

87 Senate Committee Final Report, March 10, 1998.
88 Id.
89 John Pomfret, "China Denies Contribution Charges," Washington Post, May 20, 1998.
90 www.usdoj.gov/opa/pr/2001/December/01_crm_662.htm
91 The Washington Post detailed the connections between Gore and Hsia in a February 23, 1998 piece by Robert Suro.

The nefarious connections between the Clinton-Gore team and agents of the PRC seemed to intersect with the "Buddhist Temple" fundraiser attended by Vice President Gore in April, 1996. The Taiwan-born Hsia began her relationship with Al Gore in 1988 when he was a U.S. Senator from Tennessee. She enticed him to visit Taiwan with the vague promise of future political support and the two began an eight-year relationship.[92]

Gore said his dealings with Hsia were strictly business in nature, but at one point Gore sent a letter to Hsia and Howard Hom (one of her business partners) thanking them for their support after his son had suffered a serious injury and calling them "very special friends."

Their relationship ended when she was charged with money-laundering in early 1998. The Justice Department alleged Hsia facilitated $100,000 in illegal contributions to the 1996 Clinton-Gore reelection campaign through her efforts at the Hsi Lai Buddhist Temple in California. Hsia was eventually convicted of five counts of illegal fundraising by a California jury in March 2000.[93]

The Democratic National Committee eventually returned the money donated by the Temple's monks and nuns. Twelve nuns and employees of the Temple refused to answer questions by pleading the Fifth after being subpoenaed to before Congress.[94] Two other Buddhist nuns admitted destroying lists of donors and other documents related to the controversy because they felt the information would embarrass the Temple. A Temple-commissioned videotape of the fund raiser also went missing and the nuns' attorney claimed it may have been shipped off to Taiwan.[95]

Vice President Gore said he had no idea the Temple meeting was financial in nature: "I did not know that it was a

92 Id.
93 Michael Eskenazi, "For Both Gore and GOP, A Guilty Plea to Watch," cnn.com, March 3, 2000.
94 Abse, "A Look At the 94...", Washington Post.
95 "Buddhist Nuns Admit To Destroying Documents," cnn.com, September 4, 1997.

fund-raiser. But I knew it was a political event, and I knew there were finance people that were going to be present, and so that alone should have told me, 'This is inappropriate and this is a mistake; don't do this.' And I take responsibility for that. It was a mistake."[96]

The Final Report of Governmental Affairs Committee indicated that investigators did not buy Gore's story. "The Vice President's staff knew that the Temple event was a fundraiser. In March 1996, Deputy Chief of Staff David Strauss had helped arrange a meeting in the White House with the head of the Temple, Master Hsing Yun – a meeting which Strauss believed would 'lead to a lot of $.' The White House staff repeatedly referred to the event as a 'fundraiser' in internal correspondence, and assigned to it a 'ticket price' of '1000-5000 [dollars per] head'."[97]

Ultimately, none of the nuns or monks from the Temple was charged with a crime; nor was anyone from the Gore campaign staff. However, Democrats were forced to return $2.8 million in illegal or improper donations gathered during the 1996 campaign, including all of the money contributed at the "Buddhist Temple" fundraiser.

STONEWALLED

Republicans had high hopes that the star-power Thompson would bring to bear in the investigation of illegal foreign money, particularly funds from a Communist country, pouring into the U.S. election process. They hoped that the Thompson hearings might attract enough media attention to expose not only the extent of foreign influence on American politics, but also the role of the Clinton Administration as well.

Those hopes were dashed when key witnesses either

---

96 *Vice President Al Gore, NBC's Today Show, January 27, 1997.*
97 *Senate Committee Final Report, March 10, 1998.*

declined to testify or fled the country.[98] Democrat Senator John Glenn was the Ranking Minority Member of the Committee.[99] He seemingly did everything he could to run a "four corner stall" on a full and fair investigation into the complicity of the Clinton White House in the Chinese scheme to influence the U.S. elections. For example, Glenn and the Democrats insisted on a December 31, 2007 deadline for the Committee to complete its work.

The Final Report of the Governmental Affairs Committee specifically pointed to that deadline as creating an impediment to the ability to fully and completely investigate the matter. "This deadline essentially invited witnesses and organizations to refuse to comply with subpoenas. The deadline also encouraged other witnesses and organizations, particularly the White House and the DNC, to produce documents and videotapes responsive to Committee subpoenas in a slow, drawn out manner in an effort to run the clock out on the Committee's investigation."[100]

In October, 1998 the Clinton Administration allowed the 77 year old Glenn to return to space as a member of the Space Shuttle Discovery crew, ostensibly to study the effects of space on the elderly. Many saw it as a reward for his efforts in shielding the White House from the Senate investigation.[101]

Following months of investigation, the Senate hearings began on July 8, 1997 with a day devoted largely to public statements by the Committee members. Thompson laid out his perspective of the investigative reports on that day: *"The*

98 A House Governmental Affairs Committee that investigated the same campaign finance scandal published a list of 94 key witnesses who had pled the Fifth, fled the country to avoid questions and/or prosecution or otherwise refused to answer questions from investigators. Nathan Abse, "A Look At the 94 Who Aren't Tallking," Washington Post, June 9, 1998.

99 Glenn himself had been tainted with a campaign finance investigation as one of five U.S. Senators caught up in the Keating Five scandal. Charles Keating, a savings and loan mogul, gave Glenn a $200,000 contribution that a Senate commission ultimately found reflected "poor judgment" on Glenn's part but no criminal wrongdoing.

100 Senate Committee Final Report, Section 2, March 10, 1998.

101 www.cnn.com/SPECIALS/1998/06/glenn/skeptics/

committee believes that high-level Chinese government officials crafted a plan to increase China's influence over the U.S. political process. The committee has identified specific steps taken in furtherance of the plan. Implementation of the plan has been handled by Chinese government officials and individuals enlisted to assist in the effort. Activities in furtherance of the plan have occurred both inside and outside of the United States. Our investigation suggests that the plan continues today. Although most discussions of the plan focuses on Congress, our investigation suggests it affected the 1996 presidential race and state elections as well. The government of China is believed to have allocated substantial sums of money to achieve its objectives. Another aspect of the plan is remarkable because it shows that the PRC is interested in developing long-term relationships with persons it has identified as up and coming government officials at state and local levels. The intent is to establish relations that can be cultivated as the officials rise through the ranks to higher office."[102]

Glenn, however, chose to promote the view of the Clinton White House that the Chinese only targeted congressional races and were not interested in the presidential contest: "According to the press the Chinese government intended to use a relatively modest amount of money to gain influence in the Washington lobbying game, and it intended to do this by focusing on the legislative branch of government. Now, I mention these reports here because I am greatly concerned about how the reports are sometimes discussed by individuals in this body and in the press. I've heard language like infiltration, foreign spies, foreigners, as we're jeopardizing our national security. Well, on this issue the committee should go just as far as the facts take us, recognizing that it's the FBI that's in a much better position to—than a congressional committee—to do an espionage investigation. Now, let's be careful, however, not to jump to conclusions that treason has been committed based on a partial story with ambiguous information. But wherever the trail leads let's look at it. And we want to do it fairly."[103]

Glenn then went on to surprise Thompson and the

102 www.pbs.org/newshour/campaign/july97/hearing_7-8.html
103 Id.

Republican Committee members by announcing that one of
the key players in the scheme, John Huang, would testify if
given limited immunity. The fact that Glenn was not being
cooperative in sharing information with the Committee
leadership caught Thompson off guard, and only served to
increase the acrimonious nature of the hearings.[104] As the final
deadline loomed and witnesses avoided testimony or fled the
country, it became clear that the hearings would not produce
the results many expected.

After the hearings ended and the Final Report had been
issued, Fox News Channel's Brit Hume described Thompson as
"flying high before his hearings… and shot down once they
started and all the way through them." Thompson himself
admits disappointment in the fact that the Committee did not
have as much success in ferreting out corruption as he would
have liked, and that the bi-partisan efforts that were brought to
bear during the Watergate Hearings were missing in this round.

As the investigation was consistently delayed and diverted
by the Democrat leadership, it is likely that Thompson might
have, at least once, looked around the Senate Hearing room to
wonder whether a modern version of Howard Baker might
emerge from that "other" side of the room. Someone more
intent on serving their country and seeking the truth, no matter
where it led, rather than surrendering to partisan impulses to
"protect my own President" at all costs. Ultimately, it never
happened.

Thompson says: "The congressional investigative function
is not a prosecutorial function" and acknowledges that the
hearings produced "mixed result in many respects." He believes
the criticism stems from the fact that "few people went to jail"
as a result of the Senate hearings, although criminal

---

104 *Thompson was not the only one successfully "stonewalled" by the Clinton White House.
    Clinton's FBI Director Louis Freeh, the head of the Justice Department's campaign
    finance tax force Charles La Bella and his successor Robert Conrad each recommended
    appointment of an Independent Counsel to investigate alleged abuses by Democrat
    officials and the White House. Attorney General Janet Reno refused all the requests.*

investigations by the Justice Department did lead to numerous convictions.[105]

Much of the classified information that Thompson had access to during the Committee investigation has not been made public. Based upon the conclusions reached in the Committee's Final Report it is clear that there is information contained in those classified files that provides additional proof of the involvement of the PRC and its agents in the American political process.

Thompson has seen those files, and his subsequent participation in the campaign finance reform efforts that ultimately produced the McCain-Feingold legislation was strongly influenced by his concerns over the amount of unregulated money, foreign and domestic, that was flooding into the American political system.[106] The gamesmanship that seemed to dominate business in Washington while serious issues were ignored left Thompson with a very bitter taste in his mouth. The prospect that many of the people at the center of that storm of controversy and tainted money might return to power in a Hillary Clinton White House could prove to be added incentive to propel Fred Thompson towards candidacy.

THE CLINTON IMPEACHMENT

Thompson's experiences with the "stonewalling" of his investigation into the campaign finance abuses in 1996 added to his high level of frustration with the partisan nature of business in the U.S. Senate. The willingness to put aside partisan interests in the pursuit of truth that Thompson had seen exhibited by his Republican mentor Howard Baker

---

105 Hayes, "From The Courthouse...", *Weekly Standard.* See also, www.usdoj.gov/opa/pr/2001/December/01_crm_662.htm
106 *The Bipartisan Campaign Reform Act,* known as the McCain-Feingold Act after sponsors John McCain (R-AZ) and Russ Feingold (D-WI), became law on November 6, 2002.

during the Watergate Hearings when a Republican President was the target no longer seemed to exist in Washington.

The growing disgust that Thompson felt over those who would cover for "their side" in the face of foreign campaign contributions intended to influence American policies continued to grow through the Clinton Impeachment process as partisan zeal to "get him" or "protect him" seemed to take precedence over the truth.

The Clinton Impeachment Trial in the Senate concluded February 12, 1999. A two-thirds majority vote of the Senate was needed in order to remove the President from office on either of the two charges against him: perjury and obstruction of justice. Thompson voted "no" on the perjury charge and "yes" on the obstruction of justice charge. The charge of perjury was rejected by the Senate on a 45-54 vote; the obstruction of justice vote failed 50-50. President Clinton would remain in the White House.

Thompson provided a detailed analysis of the legal and political reasons that provided the basis for his vote on the Clinton Articles of Impeachment. His comments were published in the Congressional Record on February 12, 1999.[107]

In deciding how to vote, Thompson reasoned that some acts might be illegal that are not impeachable, under the guidelines established by the Founding Fathers. Other acts might be impeachable that are not illegal, he also noted. Ultimately, while he concluded that Clinton had perjured himself, that perjury was a basis for which impeachment could be proper, but that the circumstances in this particular case did not merit removal from office because the perjury related to an essentially private matter. On the issue of obstruction of justice, however, the use of the resources and power of government by Clinton in seeking to avoid responsibility for his actions did justify a "yes" vote on impeachment for Thompson.

---

107 *On online version of Thompson's statement can be found here:*
   www.australianpolitics.com/usa/clinton/trial/statements/thompson.shtml

The failure of the Senate to deal with more pressing issues affecting the future of the country, including the threat posed by China from a military standpoint, led Thompson to begin to openly discuss whether he would seek re-election in 2002. Thompson would often quip to audiences that after a few years in Washington he had begun "to yearn for the sincerity and reality of Hollywood." There was a greater degree of seriousness underlying his comment than most might have suspected.

SEPTEMBER 11, 2001

By September 2001 it was becoming increasingly unlikely that Thompson would seek another six year term in the U.S. Senate. Then the dramatic and tragic events of September 11, 2001 unfolded. On September 24, 2001 he announced that he would in fact seek reelection, explaining that while he had considered going back into the private sector, "now is not the time to do it." "I think that there are an awful lot of Americans out there right now looking for ways to help out, and I had a pretty obvious one right here staring me in the face," Thompson explained.[108]

Thompson had begun to sound the alarm bells on terrorism long before that fateful day. But he was not anymore prepared for that day than anybody else.

When terrorists hijacked four airliners on 9/11 and attacked the World Trade Center and the Pentagon, the people around Fred Thompson saw a man ready and anxious – to help the people of his state. He was anxious because he wanted to get home to his people in Tennessee. He was anxious because his instinct was to immediately talk to as many people as possible. However, he was stuck in Washington as air traffic across the nation was halted.

He was finally able to get back home to Tennessee soil the

108 NewsHour with Jim Lehrer, September 24, 2001, pbs.org.

Saturday evening after the terror attacks. His first public act was to walk into the Two Rivers Baptist Church in Nashville on Sunday morning.

Bob Davis, now the head of the Tennessee Republican Party, was then serving as Thompson's state director. Davis had contacted Pastor Jerry Sutton via phone to request the opportunity for the Senator to speak to the congregation. Davis recalls telling Thompson that Pastor Sutton would be glad to give him "three or four minutes to speak." After a long silence on the other end of the phone, Thompson came back in his drawl and said: "I'm gonna' need a little more time than that."

Indeed, he took a lot more than "three or four minutes."

His words were needed by the 2,000-plus crowd packed into the Two Rivers Baptist Church that morning and broadcast to a Sunday morning television audience in Nashville. His words were desperately needed by a community, and a nation, that remained scared, hurt, angry and sad from the terror attack that had left nearly 3,000 dead.

He started slowly, referring only to a few hand-written notes jotted on a small piece of paper. "I know of no time when matters of the spirit and matters of public policy ought to be more together than at this time," Fred said from the pulpit.

Yes, we were all stunned by the attacks. "We're reminded of the fragility of life. We're reminded of the vulnerabilities of open societies." He paused and continued: "And we are once again reminded of the depths to which evil can go."

He encouraged people not to lose their faith in God... or in humanity. "It is important that we hold on to, as never before, our faith in God, and our faith that everything is going to be all right," he said. "Because my friends, everything is going to be all right."

Good things will come out of this horror, he told the

audience. "We will not cower, we will not hide," he said. "We will continue on."

And Fred Thompson's talk – equal measures of tough and soothing – after 9/11 showed his presidential timber. At that moment in time he didn't know or care that he was being presidential. He just said what he was moved to say.

Looking back, one wonders what might have happened if instead of just talking like a president, he was the one in charge. He called for additional funding to combat terrorism, of course, on defense, intelligence, investigations and "common-sense things."

The federal government, he said, must be more forthcoming with Americans about the extent of various terrorist threats to the United States. "We need to be frank — we're living in a different world now, and, my friends, it is a dangerous world," he said. "There are growing nuclear capabilities out there among countries that can't even feed themselves. They have declared war on us and did so some time ago, and we have been lax about saying so."

In various speeches all over the country, well before 9/11, Fred Thompson was sounding the alarm about an impending danger that was lurking not too far in the future. He had told a gathering in Savannah, Georgia in May, 2000: "We have won the Cold War, and we do not face the threat of a belligerent USSR, [but] their place has been taken by a dozen small rogue nations that are rapidly developing nuclear, biological and chemical weapons..."

He warned graduates of the University of Tennessee in Knoxville about the world's uncertainties in a 1997 commencement speech. He also sounded the alarm about "those who would harm America" in 1997 in speeches he gave in both Washington and Indiana.

Long before Fred Thompson starred in the blockbuster

television hit series *Law & Order*, he was preaching about the need for law and order in a global sense.

"He's a law and order guy," Davis said, who recalled the speeches when Fred was sounding the alarm about attacks in the future. "The show fits. He does the right thing when nobody's looking and he says the right thing even though it might not be popular. That's who he is."

During an October 2001 roundtable with security experts at the Heritage Foundation think tank he reminded attendees of the warning signs that had pointed to the 9/11 terror attacks.

"We've been told time and time again by one commission after another about the world, about the people, about the nature of the threat," Thompson said. "Maybe this time, somebody will take it to heart."

In fact, not long before 9/11 Thompson had proposed a plan that would have helped quell smugglers from sneaking weapons of mass destruction into the United States. It lost – only 17 of Thompson's colleagues in the Senate voted for it.

"I guess it's the nature of democracy; perhaps we have to be told so often and so loudly and then something has to happen before it really takes hold," Thompson said during the Heritage Foundation event.

He did not waste time after 9-11 playing the typical Washington "blame game." He dove into his job as a Senator in order to find solutions. One of his first acts after 9/11 was to ensure that the nation's computer system was secure so that rogue agents could not launch "an electronic Pearl Harbor," a sneak hack-attack against the nation's computer-reliant defenses.

Thompson was also reluctant to embrace some of the knee-jerk responses proposed in the Senate in the wake of 9-11. At a hearing of the Senate Governmental Affairs Committee on

October 4, 2001, Thompson sounded a skeptical note about the prospect of successfully reorganizing the federal homeland security bureaucracy. "The government, basically, cannot manage large projects very well," he said. "Maybe we can learn from our past experience with other government agencies and other crises and things of that nature and not make the same mistakes as we go about trying to rearrange these boxes and decide who reports to who and who has what authority. And maybe we'll take the lessons that we've learned from our other management problems in particular."[109]

In the final months of 2002, Thompson would focus his efforts on legislation that would create the Department of Homeland Security. He fought efforts by Democrats to subject the new workforce to union and collective bargaining rules that apply to federal employees more broadly. The bill passed two weeks after the 2002 midterm elections, on a vote of 90-9.[110]

"This is the most significant thing I've been involved in and certainly the most significant thing I've had my name on because it involves the main function of government, and that is protecting its citizens."[111]

"I think people are looking for someone, who, when you put your head on your pillow late at night, no matter what happens, he's going to protect your backside," Davis says. "People trust this guy. Big time." And they should.

THE DEATH OF A DAUGHTER

On January 30, 2002, Fred Thompson's focus on the national tragedy of 9-11 suddenly turned to the painful personal tragedy of the loss of his daughter Betsy. Elizabeth "Betsy" Panici died from a brain injury caused by cardiac arrest after six days at Vanderbilt Medical Center in

---

109 Hayes, "From the Courthouse...", Weekly Standard.
110 Id.
111 Id.

Nashville. She was only 38.

Panici had battled depression for many years and had
become addicted to painkillers prescribed to help her deal with
those issues. In late January, she had slipped into a coma
induced by an overdose of drugs and then her heart gave out.
There was no suicide note and the Nashville medical examiner
ruled that it was an accident.

Her brother, Tony Thompson, has said the family was
devastated by her death. "My sister had struggled for years with
an addiction to painkillers, but she had been doing really well
for some time before she relapsed. Her body couldn't cope with
the medication."[112]

Thompson was crushed by the loss of his daughter, who had
often campaigned with him. Just one month later he
announced that he had changed his mind about seeking
reelection to the Senate. "I simply do not have the heart for
another six-year term."[113]

Thompson indicated that he had considered seeking re-
election and staying in office for "a year or two." "But it quickly
became obvious that was not the right thing to do, having
somebody appointed successor and walking away in the middle
of a term. It was obvious I needed to bite the bullet now, or I
needed to serve another six-year term," he said.[114]

"For me, the George Washington example of serving eight
years and riding out of town on a horse and never returning has
great appeal." He promised to keep his hand in politics, teach a
bit, write his memoirs and return to his career in acting.[115]

As he explained his reasons for not seeking another term,

112 Sarah Baxter, "'Fred For President' Chorus Grows," *The Sunday Times*,
       April 15, 2007.
113 Bonna deLa Cruz, "Thompson Won't Run Again," *Tennessean*, March 9, 2002.
114 Id.
115 Id.

Thompson cited his growing intolerance for waiting around the Capitol until 10 at night to vote on some meaningless resolution that "has no relevance to anything that's supposed to be a part of our job." But Thompson also criticized the media for the intrusive coverage of politicians' private lives, particularly the attention on his daughter's use of drugs.

"Every public official has to understand that he or she is a public official, and that's the price you pay. For the most part, that's appropriate," he said. "That's the price your whole family pays. There are lines to be drawn. I think it's extremely unfortunate, and uncalled for, when the local newspaper discuss the details of this. Her death obviously played in my decision, but the details of all of that, what news value does that have? Why did she have to pay that price? Why does her little five-year-old boy have to pay that price because her daddy chose to try to serve his state and his country? It's over the line and more like the *National Enquirer*-type stuff than anything else."

"If a public official's kid gets in trouble, they understand it'll be treated differently, and appropriately so. But there comes a point where from a legitimate news standpoint where a little more discretion ought to be exercised. Public officials have to have thick skin, but the news media has a responsibility, too. There's no need to be dredging around things after the fact that can only be harmful and punish those that think about public service."[116]

Thompson's sudden announcement that he would not seek reelection threw Tennessee politics into turmoil. The primary election date was just five months away, in August, and both parties immediately began scrambling to recruit the best available candidates.

On the Republican side, speculation immediately turned to former Republican Governor Lamar Alexander, who had later served as Education Secretary under President George H.W.

---

116 Bonna deLa Cruz, "Thompson Ponders Past, Future," *Tennessean*, March 10, 2002. Hayes, "From The Courthouse...," *Weekly Standard*.

Bush. Alexander formally announced his candidacy on April 3, 2002 from his hometown of Maryville. Conservative Republican Congressman Ed Bryant from West Tennessee also entered the sprint for the Republican nomination.[117]

Thompson did not try to influence Republican voters during the primary, despite the fact that his close friend and longtime political ally Lamar Alexander was seeking to succeed him. Alexander's fundraising and name recognition head start gave him the edge over Bryant. Conservative Republicans in the state were not convinced that Alexander would represent their views aggressively in Washington and many sided with Bryant. Ultimately, however, the former Governor won the primary by a significant, though not overwhelming, margin of 54% to 43%.[118]

The Democrats turned to Nashville Congressman Bob Clement, whose father had been Governor of Tennessee in the late 50s and mid-60s. Clement himself had been the Democrat nominee for Governor in 1994 before losing to Republican Don Sundquist. He was essentially unopposed in the Democrats' primary, but was defeated 54% to 44% by Alexander in November, 2002.

As he watched the battle for his seat and began to wind down his time in the Senate, Thompson noted that he would have no regrets about leaving Washington or the Senate. Thompson said he tries to follow the advice of fellow Tennessean (and former resident of Lawrenceburg) Davy Crockett. "Davy said 'Be sure you're right, and go ahead,' and that's what I try to do. Having been elected twice to this job is the greatest honor I could ever have, and in many respects it's the best job there is. I've never looked at politics as a lifetime endeavor, and I never will. I'm tired of being tied to someone else's schedule, for one thing. And there are too many other

---

117 Bryant had served as one of the House Managers of the Clinton Impeachment.
118 When Senator Bill Frist chose not to seek reelection in 2006 Bryant again ran for the Republican nomination. Chattanooga Mayor Bob Corker won the nomination and the Senate general election.

things in life that are fun and rewarding."[119]

Thompson would also joke that he needed to get out of the Senate and back to acting "so his thoughts on politics and other important issues can be taken seriously."

A NEW DIRECTION

Five months after the death of his daughter Thompson took himself off of countless "most eligible bachelor" lists when he married his second wife, Jeri Kehn. Fred and Jeri were married on June 29, 2002, at First Congregational United Church of Christ in Jeri's hometown of Naperville, Illinois.

In 2003, they had their first child, a daughter, Hayden Victoria Thompson. A son, Samuel Howard Thompson, was born in November 2006.

At the time they were married, Jeri, who is twenty five years younger than Thompson, was a political and media consultant at the Verner, Liipfert, Bernhard, and McPherson law firm in Washington, D.C. She had previously worked for the Senate Republican Conference and the Republican National Committee.

"Within the space of a year and a half, I experienced the ultimate tragedy and the ultimate happiness," Mr. Thompson sighs. "I count my blessings, and I have a real focused sense of purpose now."

During the twenty years he spent as a bachelor between his two marriages, Thompson was often linked to beautiful women in Hollywood, Nashville and Washington, DC. For a while he dated country music star Lorrie Morgan. Republican Senator Orrin Hatch, who served for years with Thompson and has written a few country music songs himself once remarked that

119 Larry Bivins, "Security Much On Thompson's Mind," Tennessean, June 23, 2002.

"really lovely women just seem to like Fred." "I plead guilty", Thompson says.

When Thompson met with nearly sixty member of Congress on April 18, 2007, he was asked about his colorful dating history during the period between 1985 and 2002 when he was single. "I was single for a long time, and, yep, I chased a lot of women," Thompson replied, chuckling, according to an attendee. "And a lot of women chased me. And those that chased me tended to catch me." "But everyone I knew is still a friend, and if somehow they aren't I guess we'd hear about it. I'm happy with 'my life partner' and children now."[120]

"Jeri [Thompson] is terrific and smart. She makes him smile and the kids are beautiful," said Bob Davis. "If he runs [for President], he'll sling them on his shoulders on the campaign trail — and he's got pretty big shoulders."[121]

In the final months of his U.S. Senate term in 2002, Thompson also returned to his acting career by joining the cast of the long-running NBC television series *Law & Order*, playing New York District Attorney Arthur Branch. In fact, the first couple of episodes in which Thompson appeared were shot during the August recess to accommodate the Senator's schedule.

Thompson concurrently played the same role on both the original series and a short-lived sister series *Law & Order: Trial by Jury*. Thompson has also made occasional appearances on *Law & Order: SVU* and in the pilot episode of *Conviction*. He is one of a very few actors who have played the same regular character on two different series simultaneously.

In 2006, Thompson added his commanding presence and recognizable voice to the radio airways when he signed with ABC News Radio to serve as a senior analyst and fill-in for

120 John Fund, "*Lights, Camera...Candidacy?*" *www.opinionjournal.com*,
      March 17, 2007.
121 Baxter, "'*Fred For President*'...", *The Sunday Times*.

radio legend Paul Harvey. He continues to appear in feature films in his "spare time."

Thompson has also remained active in the political arena since leaving the Senate in January, 2003. After the retirement of Supreme Court Associate Justice Sandra Day O'Connor in 2005, Thompson was asked by President George W. Bush to help shepherd the nomination of John Roberts through the Senate confirmation process.

After Chief Justice William Rehnquist passed away on September 3, 2005, the President withdrew Roberts' nomination for the O'Conner seat on the bench and announced that Roberts would instead be appointed to replace Rehnquist as Chief Justice.

Thompson, who had himself been mentioned as a potential Supreme Court nominee, successfully guided Roberts through the treacherous waters of confirmation. Roberts was sworn in as Chief Justice of the U.S. Supreme Court on September 29, 2005.

Fred also chairs of the International Security Advisory Board, a bipartisan advisory panel. The Board reports to the U.S. Secretary of State, currently Condoleezza Rice, and focuses on emerging strategic threats, particularly those involving nuclear proliferation.

A year after stepping down from the Senate, and in compliance with Senate rules, Thompson registered to lobby for a British reinsurance company, Equitas Ltd. Records filed with the U.S. Senate show that the company paid Thompson's firm $760,000 to protect its interests regarding several bills seeking to impose liability for asbestos lawsuits. The legislation died, and Thompson ended his representation of Equitas in 2007. Equitas was the only client on whose behalf Thompson registered to lobby after leaving the Senate.

"We were very satisfied with his representation," Equitas

spokesman Jon Nash has said.[122] The company, which spent $5.3 million on a team of lobbyists from eight firms from 2004 to 2006, wanted Thompson, because "we needed help in lobbying Republicans in the Senate, and in addition, as a former senator from Tennessee, he had a good relationship with the then-Majority Leader, Sen. Bill Frist."[123]

Thompson continues to defy conventional wisdom through his honesty. He disclosed on April 13, 2007 that he had been diagnosed a few years previously with a mild form of lymphoma, which is now in remission. He said he made the announcement about this form of non-lethal cancer because he wanted to "play it straight with the American people."

"Fred is sometimes criticized for going his own way," former Tennessee Senator and Ronald Reagan chief of staff Howard Baker once said of his political protégé. "But that, my friends, is one of the very qualities we most admire."

Indeed, Fred Thompson has always created his own destiny and charted his own course. It is a quality that Tennesseans – and Americans – have come to admire. Fred's straight talk and straight action has consistently demonstrated the sort of character that people usually only see in the movies — old movies — when heroes were still heroes. Perhaps that is the real Fred Factor – and the reason he can win the White House in 2008.

---

122 *Kenneth Vogel, "Law and Order Lobbying," www.politico.com, April 2, 2007,*
123 *Id.*

Section II: How the 2008 Race Unfolds

ATMOSPHERIC DISTURBANCE

Like a tornado appearing out of the blue on a perfectly clear day, Fred Thompson burst onto the 2008 presidential picture with an appearance on "Fox News Sunday" on March 11, 2007. Asked whether he was considering running for President in 2008, Thompson responded: "I'm giving some thought to it. Going to leave the door open."[124]

The timing of Thompson's appearance was fortuitous as a new poll released that same day revealed that most Republicans were not satisfied with the current choices available in the race for the Republican presidential nomination.[125] The Thompson for President buzz had actually begun bubbling for a few weeks before the *Fox News Sunday* interview. The conservative blogosphere was already abuzz after *The American Spectator* reported several weeks before that Thompson might be mulling a run for the White House. Additional Commentary on the popular grassroots website, RedState added to the online momentum among conservatives.

But what was only talk took on greater traction when *The Hill* reported that former Senate Majority Leader and Tennessee Senator Howard Baker was making calls to build support for a presidential campaign by his protégé.[126] After that story broke Baker confirmed to the Knoxville *News Sentinel*, that he had indeed encouraged Thompson to run and that Thompson "didn't tell me to stop."

---

124 *For a transcript of the entire interview, go to www.foxnews.com.*
125 *NY Times/CBS News Poll, March 7-11, 2007.*
126 *Alexander Bolton, "Another Hollywood Star Steps Forward For the GOP," The Hill, March 9, 2007.*

Within days Tennessee Republican Congressman Zach Wamp had formed a "Draft Thompson" organization and launched a website.[127] He soon announced that he more than forty members of Congress ready to meet with Thompson to encourage his candidacy and offer their support. "It is all serious business. This is no flirtation," Wamp noted, "People want someone they can trust and someone that is strong. He has charisma coming out of his ears."

Former Senate Majority Leader, and fellow Tennessean, Bill Frist also immediately jumped into action, writing in his blog that he was encouraging Fred Thompson to run. "Now is the time for big ideas... big, true conservative ideas that rise above the fray," Frist, who decided against his own White House campaign after he left the Senate, wrote. "Fred is listening. He will carefully consider running over the next several weeks."[128]

Frist had been actively organizing and planning to run when he made his January announcement that he would not seek the Republican nomination himself. Much of the campaign apparatus and expertise that Frist had assembled quickly shifted to other candidates. But Frist's political contacts and the organizational spadework he had done in key early caucus/primary states like Iowa and New Hampshire and throughout the country during his time as Majority Leader is a huge advantage to the prospective Thompson campaign. This is particularly important from the fundraising standpoint.

Many of the Frist contacts in the fundraising arena could be re-called to active duty very quickly. This gives Thompson the ability to mobilize a first-rate finance operation at a relatively late stage in the process that few, if any, candidates would enjoy. The "Frist Factor" is a key element to the "Fred Factor" that many political experts have overlooked.

The impact of a potential Thompson campaign on the prospects of other Republican hopefuls was seen immediately.

---

127 *www.fred08.com.*
128 *www.volpac.org.*

A March 22-25 Gallup Poll (conducted just a week and a half after Thompson simply opened the door to "consider" running) placed Thompson third in the Republican field behind Giuliani and McCain. He received 12% support, while Giuliani and McCain led with 31% and 22%, respectively. Former Massachusetts Governor Mitt Romney was at just 3% (with a 3% margin of error), trailing another unannounced candidate Newt Gingrich who had 8%.[129]

But the real story of the Gallup Poll was the fact that Fred seemed to take such a large chunk of support from Giuliani. Just three weeks earlier the same poll showed Giuliani with 44% — reflecting a 13% drop with Thompson in the race. Romney also took a big hit with the addition of Fred Thompson to the mix of candidates. Interestingly, McCain seemed to emerge unscathed in this first poll.

Republican Preferences: With and Without Thompson[130]		
	Without Fred (March 4)	With Fred March 25)
Giuliani	44%	31%
McCain	20	22
Thompson	—	12
Gingrich	9	8
Romney	8	3

The next major poll to show the dramatic impact of a Thompson candidacy was the Los Angeles Times/Bloomberg poll conducted in early April, 2007.[131] That poll showed both Giuliani and McCain taking a hit with Thompson's presence, with McCain suffering the most.

The results of that poll showed Giuliani maintaining front

129 www.galluppoll.com.
130 www.galluppoll.com.
131 The Los Angeles Times/Bloomberg poll contacted 1,373 adults nationwide by telephone April 5-9. Included were 1,246 registered voters, among them 557 Democratic primary voters and 437 Republican voters. www.latimes.com.

runner status with 29% of the vote; Thompson was solidly in second place with 15%; and McCain slipped to third with 12%. Romney was at 8%. The fact Thompson had moved into a solid second place in the Republican field less than a month after merely "opening the door" to a potential race while not having yet announced nor spent a dime promoting his candidacy was a testament to the Fred Factor.[132]

A NBC/Wall Street Journal poll conducted April 20-23, 2007 showed further evidence of the impact Thompson could have on the race.[133] With Thompson included in the mix of candidates. Giuliani led among Republican primary voters with 33%, McCain followed with 22%, then Thompson at 17% and Romney at 12%.

Obviously, as Thompson himself pointed out in reaction to these polls, name recognition is a huge element of early polling. Indeed, support has to be considered "soft" for any candidate in the early stages of a campaign, and that is true on both sides of the political aisle. A huge amount of uncertainty remains, and movement up and down is guaranteed as events, both planned and unplanned, unfold.

Mitt Romney, for example, has polled very well in some of the key and early primary states where he has targeted his millions in campaign funds to finance extensive organizations and media buys. His ability to leverage these investments to generate a breakout showing in one of the early straw polls or caucuses makes him a viable contender. And the impact of the "front loading" of the primary process has yet to be determined in terms of who can stay in the game, and for how long.

Success in polling and strong name recognition helps bring

---

132 A Rasmussen Reports telephone poll of 597 likely Republican primary voters released April 24, 2007 showed the continued impact of the initial Fred Thompson "boom." Giuliani polled in first with 28%, McCain second with 15%, Fred Thompson third with 12%, and Romney fourth with 10%. www.rasmussenreports.com.
133 The NBC/WSJ poll was conducted by Hart/Newhouse and polled 1004 adults nationwide. For full details of the results go to: http://msnbcmedia.msn.com/i/msnbc/sections/news/070425_NBC-WSJ_Full.pdf

in money and volunteers and enhances visibility and attracts the media attention which builds momentum. It can also serve to create the winning mantle of "inevitability" that all candidates crave. Fred Thompson made amazing progress toward that goal in just his first few weeks as a "potential" candidate.

MONEY TALKS

Money may not be able to buy love, but if you have enough of it you can sure RENT a lot of affection in politics. At least until somebody else comes along with a better offer. Early in the election process, the media and the political pundits have only two seemingly reliable guideposts to gauge how a campaign is progressing: money and polls. Of the two, money may be the more accurate indicator of progress towards victory because it requires a certain degree of support and organizational prowess to build a successful money raising team. However, fundraising reports are often deceptive – and may even hide more glaring long-term weaknesses in a campaign or candidate.[134]

Nevertheless, the first quarter fundraising reports for the 2008 Presidential race produced some surprising numbers on both sides of the political aisle. Democrat Hillary Clinton raised $26 million dollars in the first three months of 2008 to shatter all previous fundraising records – Democrat or Republican. She also moved $10 million from her Senate campaign fund to the presidential fund for a grand total of $36 million.

---

134 *In 1996 Texas Senator Phil Gram sought the Republican nomination for President. He noted early in the campaign that "the most reliable friend you can have in American politics...is ready money." He collected over $21 million for his campaign, including a $4 million haul at one dinner in Dallas. He withdrew from the race the Sunday before the Iowa caucus took place. In the 2004 race Democrat Howard Dean raised $40 million by the end of 2003, the leading fundraiser among the Democrat candidates for President. Because of that money lead he was deemed "unstoppable" -- until he finished third in the Iowa caucuses, second in New Hampshire and never made it to Super Tuesday.*

Senator Barack Obama ran a close second raising a remarkable $25.6 million raised. More importantly, almost all of Obama's money that can be spent on the *primary* while Hillary's total was somewhat inflated by funds that can only be used in the general election. In fact, nearly 27% of Hillary's total was money that must be held for the general election. By comparison, less than *one percent* of Obama's contributions were for the general election. Nevertheless, Hillary still raised $19.1 million in primary funds – a remarkable figure except for the fact that it put her in second place in primary money.

The two candidates also raised their money in ways that were a bit different. Obama raised $6.9 million online. He also generated his money from 104,000 donors, with half of them contributing online and more than half giving less than the $2,300 maximum contribution permitted under federal campaign laws. Obama can immediately go back to more than half of his donors for more money since they are under that limit. Additionally, he can go back to his "maxed out" primary donors and ask for general election contributions. He will also attract new donors for his campaign as it continues to build momentum.

Hillary raised her money primarily from a pool of donors who had a "track record" with the Clintons. She raised money from a relatively small number of donors who gave in large amounts. In fact, nearly three-quarters of her donors "maxed out."[135] Hillary will have to attract thousands of new donors to her campaign to keep pace with the Obama surge, including many givers who have long been a part of the Clinton finance machine but who have chosen not to give to Hillary early in 2007.

All of this is good news for the Obama campaign. The bad news is that Hillary Clinton has her own personal ATM machine when it comes to political fundraising: Bill Clinton. Hillary raised $50 million in an essentially uncontested Senate

---

135 *73.9% according to the analysis of the Washington Post, April 17, 2007.*

re-election campaign in New York last year, and she built a direct mail database that generated over $30 million in contributions. Most of those contributors have not donated to the Hillary Clinton presidential campaign... yet. And Bill Clinton hasn't asked them... yet. They will soon feel the strong arm of the Clinton finance machine.

Clearly, Barack Obama is a more challenging adversary than the Clintons expected. While not on their radar screen in 2006, he is now.[136] The Obama campaign has been impressive to date, but with Hillary Clinton reporting nearly $31 million in the bank at the end of March, she has about $12 million more in available funds than the $19 million Obama reported.

Former Senator John Edwards also had an impressive first quarter of fundraising, reporting $14 million raised and $10.7 million on hand. That was approximately twice the amount he collected in the first quarter the last time he ran for President and ended up as John Kerry's vice-presidential nominee.

Another impressive showing, or at least it would have been impressive in any past quarter of presidential campaign fundraising, came from New Mexico Governor Bill Richardson. He reported raising $6.2 million, a number which might have dropped jaws just four years ago. While it is not enough to challenge the front-runners in the months ahead, the $5 million he had in the bank at the end of March, 2007 is plenty to keep him in the limelight until a Democrat Vice-Presidential nominee is selected.[137]

On the Republican side, former Massachusetts Governor Mitt Romney raised $23 million dollars, including $2.5 million

---

136 *Following the Japanese attack on Pearl Harbor on December 7, 1941, the Admiral who commanded the attack (Isoroku Yamamoto) is oft quoted as prophetically saying: "I fear all we have done is awaken a sleeping giant and fill him with a terrible resolve." Perhaps the same may be said of Hillary Clinton.*

137 *Other Democrat candidates were far behind Clinton, Obama and Edwards. Senator Chris Dodd (Connecticut) finished March with $7.5 million on hand; Senator Joe Biden (Delaware) had $2.8 million; and Congressman Dennis Kucinich (Ohio) reported $164,000 available.*

he put into the campaign himself. That figure was even more impressive when compared to the "mere" $12.9 million raised by Senator John McCain, who was considered the Republican "frontrunner" just a few months earlier. Former New York City Mayor, Rudy Guiliani, who seemed to emerge as the "front-runner" early in 2007, also raised more money than McCain, reporting nearly $15 million.

Romney's fundraising prowess gained significance when the test of "primary" money was applied to the report. The vast majority of Romney's funds were "primary dollars", just like Obama's. Giuliani's numbers were slightly inflated by donors who had already contributed to his general election campaign.[138] That general election money helped these candidates give the impression that they were in better shape financially than they actually were. But none of them will ever get to utilize that general election pool of funds unless they first win the primary.

Like Hillary, many of Giuliani's donors have already "maxed out" while Romney and McCain can still get more money from existing donors. 63.7% percent of Giuliani's reported contributors in the first quarter gave the maximum $2,300 donation.[139] Romney and McCain each reported that less than half of their own donors are barred from further primary contributions.

Another test that has to be applied to fundraising includes "cash on hand." The "burn rate" in a Presidential campaign is high. Waging a national campaign is a very expensive proposition. It costs a lot of money to raise money, create a national organization, and maintain that organization. Campaigns "burn" through money quickly, and not always efficiently. Each of the campaigns had already spent millions of dollars by the end of the first quarter of 2007, with some having a lot more to show for those expenditures than others.

---

138 *7.7% according to analysis by the Washington Post, April 17, 2007.*
139 *Washington Post, April 17, 2007.*

For example, Mitt Romney reported having $11.9 million in primary funds in the bank at the end of the first quarter, while Rudy Giuliani was close behind with $10.8 million in primary money available. John McCain was the big loser, not only because he lagged behind the other two candidates in total fundraising but because of the heavy spending by his campaign during the first quarter of the year. He reported cash on hand of only $5.2 million, along with $1.8 million in debts, leaving him with less than half the money of his chief opponents.[140]

McCain had spent $8.4 million in the first quarter alone and political pundits were properly questioning what he had gained from that spending. Likewise, Romney had spent $11.6 million, significantly more than the $5.7 million spent by Giuliani – but Giuliani's spending was enough to keep him positioned atop the list of Republican candidates in most national polls, while Romney lagged far behind. To Romney's credit, much of his spending had targeted the early caucus and primary states where his poll numbers showed results in terms of his competitiveness with Giuliani and McCain.

As these first quarter fundraising reports were released, Fred Thompson was quickly emerging in second or third place in most of the national polls, despite not having raised or spent *any* money on the race. He ranked ahead of Romney, for example, in virtually every national poll and in polls covering several key early primary states.

The question on the mind of many pundits and political experts analyzing the prospects of a Thompson candidacy is whether Thompson can raise the money and catch up should he get into the race. However, the real question should be whether or not he is really that far behind. When cash on hand totals are analyzed it is clear that he is not.

---

140 *Other Republican hopefuls were scrambling for money with comparatively meager results by the end of March, 2007. Senator Sam Brownback (Kansas) reported that he had $807,000 on hand; former Arkansas Governor Mike Huckabee claimed $374,000; Congressman Duncan Hunter (California) banked $273,000; former Wisconsin Governor Tommy Thompson had $140,000; and former Virginia Governor Jim Gilmore only had $90,000 available to his campaign.*

More importantly, Thompson has attracted more attention and communicated his ideas and issues more effectively than any of the other announced candidates while remaining on the sidelines. He can expect to raise comparable amounts of money very quickly once he gets into the Presidential race, but he will have the advantage of having started his "official" campaign from a much stronger name recognition and polling position than just about any other candidate on the Republican side of the ballot. Thompson will have positioned himself to get a much bigger "bang for his buck" by compressing the campaign time line and targeting his spending in the key primary states at a time when the voters are actually paying attention.

HONEYMOON PERIOD

Everybody loves the second-string quarterback...until he throws that first interception, gets sacked or fumbles. Fred Thompson certainly has the opportunity to fill a gaping void in the Republican Primary contest, but he will also face a tough transition from standing on the sidelines to playing in the game, if past history is any guide. If he can build on the foundation of support that he has as a "non-candidate" and gain momentum in the "entry process", which was successfully accomplished by Barack Obama on the Democrat side, then he could quickly pass McCain in the polls and be in a roughly equal position with Giuiliani by the fall.

Democrat strategist Susan Estrich has called this period Thompson's "golden moment" and encouraged him to savor it.[141] "A candidate never looks as good as he does the day before he gets in the race," Estrich writes. "If Rudy Giuliani weren't running, everyone would be saying, 'we need Rudy.' If John McCain had decided to sit this one out, the conventional wisdom would be that he was the guy who might be best able to pull this off. If Mitt Romney had decided to stay out, the press

---

141 Susan Estrich, *"Fred Thompson Should Enjoy Golden Moment,"* www.foxnews.com, May 2, 2007.

would be painting him to be a prince instead of a poor waffler. In Democratic circles, all the talk about Al Gore as the potential savior ignores the fact that eight years ago, Democrats couldn't shut up about what a terrible candidate he was."[142]

Fred Thompson can certainly make that transition if he enters the race, but it is a challenge for any candidate and many have stumbled out of the blocks. Yet, the patient and step-by-step approach that Thompson exhibited in the early weeks and months of the non-campaign revealed a steadiness that will be valuable when the real "fire fight" of presidential politics begins.

CONSERVATIVES UNITE

One of the key initial tests, and opportunities, for Fred Thompson could come in Iowa, and his decision of whether or not to compete in the Iowa straw poll in August, 2007.

Iowa voters always get a good look at all the candidates during the course of the campaign. The Iowa caucuses provide the "up close and personal" contact with the potential Presidential nominees that voters in other states (except New Hampshire) seldom, if ever, experience. All of the major candidates will make dozens of trips to Iowa before the actual caucus votes are cast on January 14, 2008. Republican candidates, however, have a big date in Iowa long before the caucus vote.

On Saturday, August 11, 2007, Iowa Republicans will gather in Ames, Iowa at the Iowa State University campus to select their preferred Republican candidate for President. Those who pay to attend this Iowa Republican Party fundraising event (or who have a campaign pay for their ticket) and have a valid Iowa driver's license will be allowed to vote in the straw poll. The results will give a big boost to the winner

---

142 Id.

and pull the rug from under any "front-runner" who fails to meet expectations.

In 1999, then Texas Governor George W. Bush made his first campaign visit to Iowa in June and announced that he would not only compete in the straw poll, but that he would win. He did; and went on to win the Iowa caucus, the Republican nomination, and the Presidency. That same year, now-Tennessee Senator Lamar Alexander and former Vice President Dan Quayle saw their own presidential hopes dashed by "back in the pack" finishes in the straw poll. Both of them ended their campaigns soon after.[143]

Thompson is in a different situation from many of the candidates, in that as of late April, he was still speaking with advisers and holding what he called a "dialogue with the American People" over a potential run. Participating in the Ames straw poll takes money, and already so-called "top tier" Republican candidates have spent hundreds of thousands of dollars to lock up commitments from local Hawkeye State balloteers.

To get an idea of how much it costs to play in the Iowa straw poll, consider that in 2000, Steve Forbes spent an estimated $2 million for his statewide poll operation. And that investment got him a close second place finish in the vote. Already, McCain and Romney have committed large sums to the Iowa straw poll, and other candidates, such as Senator Sam Brownback are looking to build a reputation on their straw poll performance.

On the other hand, Thompson could adopt the tactic that Rudy Guiliani may be following and choose not to participate in the straw poll. If two of the major players, Thompson and Guiliani, both sit it out, then whatever benefit might otherwise attach to the winner becomes less significant. Others might also

---

143 *Only 23,685 total votes were cast in the 1999 straw poll, which Bush won with 31%. Steve Forbes and Elizabeth Dole finished second and third, with 21% and 14% respectively.*

follow suit, particularly if it causes some of the "back in the pack" candidates to spend a lot of precious time and money on a hollow victory.[144]

The key to such a decision is continuing to show respect for the voters, not only of Iowa, but across the country. Giuliani has visited Iowa on campaign swings. No doubt, candidate Fred Thompson would make similar forays into the first caucus state in the nation. His commanding physical presence, celebrity status, and common sense approach to the issues will play particularly well in a setting where the "personal touch" matters.

It is a giant chess game, and all the major candidates will be trying to make the others blink first — and make a move that, in hindsight, will clearly be the wrong one. With several big states moving their primary dates up to February, the money and staffing resources necessary to win in the straw poll in Iowa may be more wisely expended elsewhere.[145] All of the major campaigns will be making that calculation right up until the weeks before the straw poll.

But regardless of how Thompson plays the Iowa Straw Poll, he remains perfectly positioned to gather the support of Republican voters who are not yet firmly (or in some cases even "softly") committed to any of the other candidates. Some of these voters are not comfortable with the less-than-conservative credentials of the two perceived front-runners: former New York City Mayor Rudy Guiliani and Arizona Senator John McCain. Even though they greatly admire his

---

144 In 1999, Senator John McCain skipped both the Iowa straw poll and the caucus itself, calling the straw poll a "sham." This time he is focusing both time and money on an effort to win the same "sham" straw poll.

145 Republican voters will head to the polls in South Carolina on February 2. (Democrats will hold their primary in South Carolina on January 29.) But the big battle looms on February 5. About 20 states including Florida, California, Colorado, Georgia, Missouri, North Carolina, New Jersey, New York, Utah, Tennessee, Texas and Illinois, will conduct their primary election on that day. By the evening of February 5 more than half the delegates to the Republican Convention will have been decided. The continued "front loading" of the primaries will have a huge impact on the political process in 2008 and elevates the advantage of Fred Thompson's celebrity appeal.

leadership qualities, Republican conservatives have serious problems with Guiliani's anti-gun, pro-gay, pro-abortion track record. McCain has not been a reliable conservative, and is distrusted by many.

Others find that the conservative candidates that they prefer don't seem to have great prospects for winning the Republican nomination (e.g. Senator Sam Brownback, Congressman Duncan Hunter, and former Arkansas Governor Mike Huckabee) due to lack of resources and name recognition. And finally, there are those who are energized by the strategic and intellectual talents that former House Speaker Newt Gingrich could bring to the race, however, they have grave doubts about his electibility in the general election.

A March 2007 poll of Republican voters revealed that 57% wanted more choices than they had available in the Republican presidential primary.[146] That same poll indicated that 73% of Republican Primary Voters believed it was more important to vote for a candidate with whom they agree on most of the issues rather than someone who can "win in November."[147] Republicans want to win in November 2008, but they want the right candidate to carry their standard to victory.

The populist appeal of Fred Thompson is undeniable; it has fueled a firestorm of interest in his candidacy from the moment he first considered running. Conservatives hungry for a consistent conservative with the charisma to communicate his views clearly find a Thompson campaign appealing. That gives him the opportunity to unite conservatives behind him.

Many within the conservative core of the Republican Party have been disappointed with what they have viewed as abandonment of key conservative principles by the Bush Administration. The drumbeat of failure pounded home by the mainstream media in covering the War in Iraq has certainly not

146 *Question 73, NY Times/CBS News Poll, March 7-11, 2007, sampling 1,362 adults nationwide, including 698 Republicans.*
147 *Question 60, id.*

helped, neither has the inability of the White House to explain not only the *need* to produce victory in Iraq, but the *path* to getting there. The steady drip-drip of casualty reports from Iraq has emboldened those who attack American forces on the battlefield, as well as those who attack America's Iraq policy here at home.

The President's low approval numbers have been a product of the Left who hate him combined with a Republican base that no longer support him. The poor job approval ratings that President Bush has garnered from Democrats and Independents are not surprising. What has pushed him to record low levels, however, is a direct by-product of *Republicans* who do not support him. If he just had relatively decent support from his own party, his approval numbers could be ten points higher – in the historical range enjoyed by most Presidents.

In fact, despite all the problems that the Bush Administration experienced during the first term, President Bush had actually climbed back to a nearly even approval/disapproval split in daily Rasmussen Reports poll numbers in February, 2006.[148] That's when the Dubai Ports deal came to light.

Although the Dubai Ports deal actually involved a change in the management of the U.S. port facilities rather than actual "sale of the ports", the deal seemed to underscore the weakness of the Bush Administration in protecting the borders of the United States. It allowed those who opposed the deal to raise concerns among citizens, not only about security at home, but also the specter of a new, potential terrorist threat through shipping lines, and lack of accountability for decisions made in several Bush Administration departments: the State Department, the Treasury Department and the Department of Homeland Security.

In less than a week the President plummeted back down to

---

148 *www.rasmussenreports.com.*

the forty percent range in approval in the Rasmussen polling, numbers that were also reflected in other national polls. By the time the deal was cancelled, the damage to Bush's poll numbers was complete, he has never recovered.

For many conservatives, compounding the picture of a porous port system was the Administration's decision to take on once again the issue of immigration reform, further reminding the public about the President's failure to secure America's borders from the continuing flood of illegal aliens. A renewed push for "amnesty" for illegals only served to compound the President's problems with his base.

Bush's problems with the conservative Republican base go beyond the hot button issue of illegal immigration. The reckless and profligate spending throughout his term in office symbolized by the "Bridge to Nowhere" and his anemic response to relentless partisan attacks brought a demoralized Republican Party to the polls in November, 2006.[149] With the anchor chain of the Bush Administration around their necks Republican candidates were drowned in a sea of disaffected voters who handed power to the Democrats in both the House and Senate.

Candidates perceived by conservatives as too slick or too shifty simply won't be trusted to keep their word after the collective experience of the past six years. A straight talking, principled conservative like Fred Thompson seems the perfect person to fill the void. Clearly, voters are hungry, if not starving, for someone with his track record of fighting corruption, telling it like it is, and refusing to back down. Fred Thompson satiates that appetite.

---

149 *In 2005 Congress approved three separate "earmarks" in a highway bill to build a bridge in Ketchikan, Alaska (population 8,900) to connect it to the town of Gravina (population 50). Dubbed the "Bridge to Nowhere", the total cost was to be $320 million in taxpayer dollars. It became a symbol of fiscal irresponsibility and wasteful spending by a Republican-controlled House and Senate. For background go to: www.heritage.org/Research/Budget/wm889.cfm*

RIDING THE WAVE

After merely opening the door to considering a run for President, Fred Thompson created a sudden and dramatic wave of immediate momentum that allowed him to rise to the top tier of candidates. Critical for Thompson will be the development and implementation of a successful strategy to ride the initial wave of support, and the much bigger wave that could be created by the method and timing of an actual announcement. Otherwise, the Thompson "spring offensive" could end up being nothing more than an interesting footnote in political history.

Because of Thompson's radio and television commitments, he may not be able to formally initiate a campaign until June of 2007. Thompson is a star in NBC's "Law and Order" series, and the important ratings "sweeps" period in May could keep him on the air and out of the political race until the season ends.

Under federal campaign laws requiring "equal time" for candidates on the public airwaves, a Fred Thompson appearance in a movie or television show could require a television station to provide the same amount of time on air for the other Republican candidates. These rules, enforced by the Federal Communications Commission (FCC), do not apply to candidate appearances on newscasts, interview programs or news events. But the rules have been applied to television and movie stars who have become candidates in the past.

When Arnold Schwarzenegger ran for California Governor in 2003, television stations dropped all his movies out of fear that showing them would allow the other 134 candidates to ask for equal time on the air. Stations also pre-empted Ronald Reagan's movies when he ran for Governor and later President.

The FCC rules have never been applied to cable television, which is where most of the reruns of "Law and Order" air in syndication. However, cable stations might choose to voluntarily abide by the equal time guidelines to avoid a lawsuit that might produce a legal ruling forcing them under FCC rules in the future. Only the time that Thompson actually appears on air counts for purposes of calculating equal time; and, it is up to the competing campaigns to monitor the airwaves and make their demand for air time within seven days.

Even if Thompson announces that he's getting in the race, the equal-time provisions — and the blackout for the reruns of his television shows and movies — do not automatically nor immediately kick in.[150] The law applies only to "legally qualified" candidates – meaning those whose names appear on official state ballots rather than people who have simply announced a campaign. So even after Thompson announces his "intention" to run and starts campaigning, he may continue to appear on television screens throughout the country – getting more visibility than his opponents can possibly afford to purchase.

Once Thompson does take the step of announcing his "intent" to run, the impact will be immediate. Several campaigns that are in the formative stage and are based on becoming the consensus choice of the conservative base in the Republican Party may end at that point. Kansas Senator Sam Brownback, former Virginia Governor Jim Gilmore and former Wisconsin Governor Tommy Thompson are among those who will feel the pressure to close their operations.[151]

Others may seek to hold on until the Iowa Straw Poll in August in the hope that lightning may strike and a better than expected finish will energize their efforts. Former Arkansas Governor Mike Huckabee, has realistically noted that if he cannot finish in the top four in Iowa in August he will be out. If both Thompson and Giuliani skip that Iowa Straw Poll it

---

150 Michael D. Shear, "Fred Thompson's Presidential Hopes Could Put 'Law' Reruns In Lockup," Washington Post, March 30, 2007.
151 Congressmen Duncan Hunter (CA) and Tom Tancredo (CO) have a presence in the presidential race primarily founded upon their support for immigration reform. Their presence in the race will keep pressure on the top tier candidates to embrace border security and enforcement of immigration laws, but it is highly unlikely that either emerges as the nominee.

makes a top four finish essentially meaningless.

Ultimately, only three other candidates are likely to survive an initial Thompson surge and remain as viable prospects for the Republican nomination: Giuliani, Romney and McCain. Giuliani has the national name recognition, financial support and organizational capacity to wage a fight for the Republican nomination until it is finally won, by him or someone else. His leadership skills are unquestionable, and his strength and toughness are qualities that American voters respect and admire. The fact that millions of us feel comfortable referring to him as simply "Rudy" reveals a shared and personal connection with him. That familiarity is rooted in the events of 9-11 when he strode boldly into the public consciousness of so many who had never known much about him before that horrible day. He is truly "America's Mayor."

Rudy's extraordinarily high name recognition and celebrity status has made him the initial front-runner. As primary voters become more engaged in the process, they will focus on his positions in regards to social policies. These positions seem to be in direct opposition to the majority of voters, which could cause his support to wane.

Romney has raised a phenomenal amount of early money, has plenty on hand, and has the personal funds available to continue even if his fundraising efforts slow down. Romney has the added advantage of possessing "executive experience." Experience as a Governor has certainly been helpful to other presidential aspirants in the recent past.[152] His successes outside the realm of politics also give him a compelling story to tell, and he tells it well. In fact, Mitt Romney has all the attributes that define someone as the kind of person who "should" be President, including the fact that he really doesn't need the job.

However, despite the planning and organization that has

---

152 *For example, former Governors Reagan, Carter, Clinton and George W. Bush, all of whom ended up in the White House.*

put Romney in the thick of the Republican presidential race, his campaign must quickly move into high gear, or the entry of Fred Thompson into the race will suck the air out of his campaign. The "front loaded" primary process will make it even more difficult for Romney to win. His strategy seems to depend upon getting "better than expected" results in Iowa or New Hampshire and then build upon that success in later primary states. That strategy has worked out in the past, but the rapid pace of the primaries in early 2008 will complicate things for Romney.

It is not just the number of primaries that come close on the heels of New Hampshire, it is the fact that voters in so many large states like California, Illinois and Florida will head to the polls almost immediately after. Candidates will need massive sums of money for television advertising in those states, and the funding simply cannot be collected quickly enough following whatever success may be gained in Iowa and New Hampshire. Name recognition and celebrity will be a critical component in those states and Romney may not be able to get enough of it soon enough to mount effective efforts in the follow-up states, particularly when Giuliani and Thompson start with big leads in those categories.

If, however, Romney can simply "hang in" long enough for Giuliani or Thompson to knock the other out of the race he may then emerge as the only remaining option. Under those circumstances, he could still grab the nomination. Romney's prospects are better if Giuliani knocks out Thompson, or if Fred ultimately chooses not to enter the race, rather than if Giuliani is the one who falters.

McCain is in deep trouble. His poll numbers were stagnant before the Fred Thompson talk began, and slipped as the Thompson campaign moved from boomlet toward reality. His own campaign staff described his first quarter fundraising results as "disappointing." Once McCain's "cash on hand" figures were revealed in mid-April, 2007, his financial situation went from "disappointing" to potentially "disastrous." The next fundraising reports are due in mid-July, and will likely determine whether or not McCain can afford to remain in the race.

McCain's difficulties were underlined by a Fox News/Opinion Dynamics poll conducted in mid-April, 2007 that showed McCain with increasingly high negative numbers in approval-disapproval ratings.[153] McCain registered a 49-31% favorable to unfavorable split among all of those who responded, and a 60-20% split among Republicans. Giuliani, by comparison had an overall approval/disapproval rating of 55-25% and a 73-13% division among Republicans.[154] With less money available than either Giuliani or Romney, and with Fred Thompson drawing more and more of the "free media", McCain's capability to turn his slipping numbers around becomes even more difficult in the coming months.

Campaigns that are experiencing trouble often stumble over seemingly innocuous events that give the media and opponents a feeding frenzy opportunity by putting just a bit of "blood in the water." McCain did just that in an April 19, 2007 campaign appearance in South Carolina where he responded to a question about Iran by singing a few bars of the Beach Boys' tune "Barbara Ann" with the words "bomb, bomb Iran..." McCain brushed off criticism over the incident, but the liberal political organization Moveon.org immediately announced plans to spend $100,000 on an anti-McCain television campaign highlighting his joke. It is the kind of misstep that seldom derails a campaign, but does distract staff and fundraisers from the serious business of "winning an election" for a few days, and that lost time is often more critical than the

---

153 *The telephone poll was conducted April 17-18, 2007 with a total sample of 900 registered voters.*

154 *McCain could perhaps take some comfort in the fact that two other potential presidential nominees recorded much higher levels of disapproval from voters. Hillary Clinton had a 46-47% approval/disapproval response; and Al Gore received comparable ratings with a 48-41% split.*

long term damage, if any, from the actual gaffe.[155]

All of these factors combine to make it increasingly difficult for Senator John McCain to develop a "glide path" to the Republican nomination for President, regardless of whether or not Fred Thompson ultimately enters the race. But the entry of Thompson into the presidential campaign will hasten the end of McCain's bid, and many of his supporters, donors and staff are likely to move onto the Thompson camp. Depending upon the timing of a McCain exit from the race, Thompson could effectively inherit an "up and running" operation to some extent.

GIULIANI VERSUS THOMPSON

Fred Thompson poses a huge challenge to Rudy Giuliani's presidential prospects. Like Rudy, voters who come in contact with him immediately feel comfortable with calling him simply "Fred." And like Rudy, Fred has the "it" factor – that unique combination of celebrity, gravitas, charisma, and confidence that a candidate either has or lacks. Ronald Reagan had it. Bill Clinton had it. Barack Obama has it. Rudy and Fred both have it.

They are also relatively transparent men, meaning "what you see is what you get." They are who they are and they are comfortable with that—which makes others comfortable with them.

Fred and Rudy also share a common commitment to battling corruption and crime. Both men spent time as prosecutors. Each of them engaged in high profile battles for truth and justice: Rudy took on the Mob; Fred helped bring

---

155 *The incident also underlined the "youtube" impact on modern campaigning. The video clip of the McCain quip was widely circulated before the mainstream media even picked up on the story. Former Virginia U.S. Senator George Allen also got "youtubed" during his 2006 reelection bid with his "macaca" comment. "Youtube" videos, internet/blog communication, and other new technology will play a huge role in the 2008 campaign, and those candidates that best figure out how to use these avenues to the voters to their benefit, while avoiding getting burned, improve their chances of victory.*

down a corrupt Nixon Administration and a Tennessee Governor who was selling pardons and paroles. Neither has a tolerance for those who skirt the laws of our land.

The two men have a thorough intellectual understanding of the Constitutional principles that are the foundation of our Republic.[156] More importantly, they share a passion for protecting those principles.

Both men came from modest upbringings. Rudy was born in Brooklyn, New York to working class parents who were both the children of Italian immigrants. Fred was born in Sheffield, Alabama, but grew up in Lawrenceburg, Tennessee. Fred's parents were also working class folks, neither of whom graduated from high school. Both men reflect the American dream of achieving the highest levels of success through hard work and talent.

The two have dramatically different accents. Rudy shoots from the lip in the staccato rapid fire of a "New Yawker." Fred expresses himself in a slow drawl with the rounded edges of the South and a hint of the gravel of a dirt road. Both men understand the language of America, and each man gives voice to the optimistic view of this country that Reagan was always able to capture. In fact, both Rudy and Fred may make claims to being an "ideological heir" to Ronald Reagan.

But Fred has something that Rudy lacks. Fred has conservative credentials to back him up.

During his eight years in the U.S. Senate (1994-2002) Thompson compiled a lifetime rating of 86% by the American Conservative Union. Other Republicans (like Strom Thurmond, Trent Lott and Jesse Helms) earned slightly more conservative ratings than Thompson, but he was comparable to Rick Santorum (87%) and a few percentage points to the right

---

156 Both men graduated from outstanding law schools. Giuliani from New York University; Thompson from Vanderbilt University.

of John McCain (83%).[157]

Rudy recently reaffirmed his pro-Choice position on abortion, including his commitment to federal funding being used to perform abortions. When the Supreme Court upheld a nationwide ban on partial birth abortion in a 5-4 decision on April 18, Giuliani praised the decision.[158] However, he had previously indicated that he would have voted AGAINST the partial birth abortion ban that the Supreme Court approved in its April ruling.[159] Giuliani's support for abortion goes beyond policy-making as he has made financial contributions to support the practice as well. Despite saying he "abhors abortion" personally, his financial records reveal that he contributed money at least six times to Planned Parenthood during the 90s. Planned Parenthood is one of the country's leading abortion rights groups and the top provider of abortions nationally.[160]

Thompson is pro-life. He had a 100% pro-life voting record on abortion issues during his time in the Senate, including voting to ban partial birth abortion and cloning. He has said that *Roe v. Wade* is bad law and should be overturned.[161] While some of the other candidates for the Republican nomination have recently become much more pro-life in their campaign rhetoric, Thompson has consistent and long-term pro-life voting record to back up what he says on the issue. For most pro-life voters, actions are likely to speak louder than words.

On other social issues like gun-control and gay rights, including "civil unions", Rudy Giuliani has consistently taken a more liberal approach than that embraced by the conservative mainstream of the Republican Party. Even on fiscal matters Giuliani has some baggage. As Mayor of New York he helped initiate a lawsuit that gave the Supreme Court

---

157 *www.conservative.org.*
158 *The cases were Gonzales v. Carhart and Gonzales v. Planned Parenthood.*
159 *The Hill, April 18, 2007. www.thehill.com.*
160 *Jonathan Martin, "Giuliani Gave To Planned Parenthood," www.politico.com,*
     May 7, 2007.
161 *"Fox News Sunday," March 11, 2007. www.foxnews.com.*

the opportunity to strike the "line item veto" from the President's repertoire of budget cutting powers. And his legendary rebuilding efforts in New York City were largely funded by heavy taxes imposed on commuters.[162]

Fred Thompson has been a staunch supporter of the Second Amendment and compiled a Senate voting record that won consistent raves from the National Rifle Association. He opposes gay marriage and "special rights" for gays. He not only "talks the talk" as a conservative, he has consistently "walked the walk" with his votes in the U.S. Senate.

Influential social conservatives seem poised to join the Thompson bandwagon as soon as he enters the race. Richard Land, the President of the Southern Baptist Convention's Religious and Ethics Liberty Commission, has noted that the top rung of Republican presidential candidates have too many flaws for social conservatives to offer full support to any of them. Land sees Fred Thompson as the man to fill a big ideological hole in the race. "Fred Thompson reminds me of a Southern-fried Reagan," Land has said. Describing Thompson as a "masterful retail politician" he has noted that watching Fred campaign must be what it was like "to watch Rembrandt paint."[163]

The Supreme Court ruling in *Gonzales v. Planned Parenthood* affirming a ban on partial birth abortion will certainly make abortion a hot topic on the campaign trail throughout the primary process. Democrat candidates were uniform in their condemnation of the case as an assault on a woman's right to choose. Republican candidates were equally loud in praising the case. Despite Giuliani's support for the decision, it will only exacerbate his problems with social conservatives in the Republican Party. The fact that the decision came only days after Giuliani spoke at a large

---

162 Kimberly A. Strassel, *"Rudy's Big Apple Baggage,"* April 13, 2007. www.opinionjournal.com.
163 Sam Youngman, *"Evangelical Leader Warms to Run By Thompson in '08"*, April 4, 2007. www.thehill.com.

gathering of Republican faithful in Iowa and urged the Party "to get beyond social issues like abortion" could not have been worse, from a timing standpoint.[164]

Giuliani's problems with the conservative base will be further complicated by his anti-gun track record. Rudy supported the 1994 "assault weapons" ban that President Bill Clinton signed into law. As Mayor of New York, he joined in a lawsuit against firearm manufacturers to force them to pay damages suffered from criminals' use of guns. He endorsed a national gun licensing program that would have required gun owners to demonstrate good moral character and a "reason" to have a gun.[165]

Support for the 2nd Amendment will get particular emphasis from Republican primary voters in the 2008 race due to the D.C. Court of Appeals ruling in *Shelly Parker, et al. v. D.C.* which overturned the District's gun ban. Regardless of whether the Supreme Court ever hears arguments or rules on that particular case, it has moved the issue of whether the "right to bear arms" is an individual right or one limited to members of a militia to the front burner. The horrific murder spree at Virginia Tech University on April 16, 2007 will give added impetus to the controversial issue of gun control in the 2008 election process. Unfortunately for Rudy, he is on the wrong side of the "gun issue" with most Republican Primary voters.[166]

Another major issue that will undermine Rudy's appeal to conservative Republicans is his past support for illegal immigration. As Mayor of New York he often defended illegal aliens. For example, he fought federal efforts to restrict health care and education benefits for illegals, advocated creation of a $12 million city agency to help illegals gain citizenship, and

---

164 *Thomas Beaumont, "Get Past Social Issues, Giuliani Tells Backers," April 15, 2007, Des Moines Register.*

165 *Andrew Ferguson, "The Unlikely Frontrunner," The Weekly Standard, April 9, 2007.*

166 *The fact that New York City Mayor Michael Bloomberg, who followed Rudy as Mayor, helped fund and lead an anti-gun television ad campaign immediately following the Virginia Tech massacre will not be helpful to Rudy in garnering support from gun owners and the National Rifle Association.*

prevented city agencies from denying them access to taxpayer funded programs. Unlike most of the other candidates, he has a record on illegal immigration that contradicts what he is saying on the campaign trail today. It will certainly complicate things for him in the months ahead as more voters learn where he actually stands on this contentious issue.[167]

Ultimately, Fred Thompson's entry into the Republican primary race will doom Rudy Giuliani's chances. Conservative Republican primary voters who might have been willing to "hold their nose" and support Rudy (despite his socially liberal view on so many critical issues) will have a choice that does not require them to compromise their values. They don't have to choose to sacrifice their values in order to win the White House.

Rudy will be tough on terrorism, but so will Fred. Rudy has the "it" factor, name recognition and celebrity appeal that will be crucial to winning the large states that have front-loaded the primary process, but Fred has all those same qualities. But Fred is a conservative, and Rudy simply, is not.

On March 12, 2007 *Weekly Standard* Contributing Editor Noemie Emery published a column explaining how social conservatives in the Republican Party would simply have to "deal" with the socially liberal Giuliani being their standard bearer in 2008.[168] She wrote:

> "Strict conservatives are not all that enthralled by any of the three main contenders—Giuliani, John McCain, and Mitt Romney. This is their weakness, but also their strength, as they all tend to give each other cover along with other conservative stars. Did Giuliani leave his first wife? So did McCain. Did he leave his second wife? So did Newt Gingrich. Is he pro-choice and gay-friendly? So

167 Marc Santora and Sam Roberts, "Candidate Giuliani Shifts His Tone on Immigration," *New York Times*, April 22, 2007.
168 Noemie Emery, "Let's Make A Deal," *Weekly Standard*, March 12, 2007. www.weeklystandard.com.

was Mitt Romney a scant four years ago. McCain is the only one with a firm pro-life record, but the base doesn't like him for a number of reasons, among them tax cuts, immigration, campaign finance reform, and being used by the press to score points against conservatives on too many things to enumerate."

Emery concluded: *"Some day their prince may come — the conservative who hits all the bases — pro-life, pro-supply side, pro-tax cuts, pro-deregulation, and hawkish in foreign policy — but this day is not it, and that day may never arrive."*

Ironically, at perhaps the very moment she penned those words, that "prince" stepped forth in the form of Fred Thompson, and the need for social conservatives to "deal" seemed to evaporate overnight.

PICKING THE VEEP

Regardless of who wins the Republican nomination for President, the selection of a Vice Presidential nominee will be absolutely critical to success in the fall. That process will begin as early as early as mid-March 2008, by which time the vast majority of Republican Convention delegates will have been selected.

The most important factor in picking a Vice Presidential nominee should be whether or not that individual is ready and able to immediately move into the top spot if necessary. However, history tells us that this factor has seldom been considered the most important one. The ability to help secure the White House for the person who has won the nomination (or at least not doing any measurable damage to those prospects) has more often been the actual test.

There are a number of political factors that will be examined (and polled) to aid in making a final decision as to who best helps the ticket win. Does the potential Vice-presidential nominee bring any states into the Electoral Vote column that might otherwise go to the "other side?" In some cases the desire to bring not only a particular state, but an entire region, into play can dictate a choice.[169] Does the prospect bring ideological balance to the ticket? Will the addition of that person to the team bring added "gravitas" or experience that the nominee himself/herself is missing? Do the two candidates like each other, or at the very least have the ability to tolerate the other? And an element that may loom particularly large in 2008: is there a gender or ethnic reason to select someone?

The first group of potential dance partners that Fred Thompson or any other Republican presidential nominee will sort through will include those who did well in the Republican caucus/primary process. If the primary battle becomes particularly contentious there could be pressure to unite the disparate elements within the party by offering the second place finisher a spot on the ticket.

THE CONTENDERS

If Thompson is the nominee, there would certainly be some geographical balance brought to the ticket by the selection of either former Massachusetts Governor Mitt Romney or former New York City Mayor Rudy Giuliani. (Both men clearly pass the "can he be President if something happens" test.) But it is unlikely that either of them would move his own state into the Republican Electoral column.[170]

---

169 *The importance of geographical balance is clearly not essential. Arkansas Governor Bill Clinton proved that when he successfully won the Presidency after choosing neighboring state Tennessee Senator Al Gore as his running mate in 1992. And Dick Cheney was clearly not selected by Texas Governor George W. Bush in 2000 in order to insure that he "locked up" Wyoming.*

170 *Romney's father George W. Romney was once Governor of Michigan (1963-69), and Romney himself was born in the state. There may be some residual benefits to the Romney name in that state which could shift it into the Republican column.*

From a regional standpoint, either Romney or Giuliani might improve Republican prospects in the swing state of New Hampshire. Would they bring New Jersey into play? Maine, perhaps? Would someone from the Northeast slotted in the second seat actually give Republicans a chance in this "bluest of the blue" region? Probably not.

Giuliani would add some celebrity status and further enhance the "tough on terror" resume of the Republican ticket, strengths that Thompson already has.[171] He clearly has cross-over appeal to Democrats and Independents. His experience as a Chief Executive would certainly be valuable – both during the campaign and in setting up an Administration.

But the same liberal social positions that will plague him during the primary process are not likely to be easily dismissed by the conservative base if he is selected for the Vice President slot on the ticket. As "heir apparent" to the Republican nomination down the road his selection would obviously raise some concerns. Finally, is his personality suited to being the number two guy? Most, including Rudy would probably conclude "NO".

Romney brings energy, charisma and the same sort of valuable experience as a Chief Executive that Giuliani can claim. He also has a business track record that makes for a great story, but an even better foundation for ultimately governing. His intellect and strategic skills would be a huge asset to both the campaign and a Thompson Administration. He is also young enough to use his time as Vice President to set the stage for his own Administration. Some Evangelical Christians have been slow to embrace Romney's candidacy because of the so-called "Mormon issue." If Romney is slated for the second spot rather than the top spot on the ticket the issue may be less relevant.[172]

---

171 If Romney or Giuliani are the nominee would they select Thompson as their Vice President? Perhaps. Thompson has said he is not interested in the second slot, but that is what every Vice President has said at one point.

172 Talk radio host and best selling author Hugh Hewitt addresses the political impact of Mitt Romney's Mormonism in detail in his book "A Mormon In The White House?: Ten Things Every American Should Know About Mitt Romney," (2007).

But in the final analysis, Thompson might decide that Romney would be a better fit as a "superstar" in the Cabinet rather than on the ticket. With Hillary as the Democrat nominee, she will almost certainly select either Obama or Richardson as her own Vice Presidential nominee.[173] If Obama gains the nomination then the Democrats will have a historic "makeup" for their ticket regardless of who he selects as a Vice Presidential nominee. It is a virtual certainty that the Democrat ticket in 2008 will reflect gender or ethnic diversity, or both. The Republicans nominee, whether it is Thompson, Giuiliani, Romney or one of the other candidates, will find it essential to break from the "two white male" ticket composition in order to win. Romney does not accomplish that for Thompson.

All of the other contenders for the Republican nomination for President fail as picks for the second slot for the same reason. Brownback, Huckabee, Tancredo, Tommy Thompson, and Gilmore all have good qualifications and each could be effective as both a Vice Presidential candidate and eventually in the office itself. But none of them provide a counterbalance to the gender and ethnic advantages that the Democrats will possess. None of them bring states into the Republican Electoral column that Fred Thompson cannot win without them.

Adding ethnic and/or gender diversity to the Republican ticket will not be the only consideration that Thompson (or any other Republican nominee) will have to consider in sorting through prospects, but it will be a critical factor in winning or losing.[174] Unfortunately, the Republican cupboard is somewhat

---

173 *If former Vice President Al Gore enters the race for the Democrat nomination late in 2007 he will be a formidable challenge for Hillary. See, Tim Shipman, "Gore Campaign Team Assembles in Secret", The Sunday Telegraph, April 21, 2007. www.telegraph.co.uk. If he runs and doesn't beat her, he would certainly be a strong prospect for her number two spot. But would Gore want to be Vice President for another Clinton? Not likely; and he would definitely not select her if he secures the nomination himself.*

174 *One "white male" that might make sense would be Senator Joe Lieberman of Connecticut. He would put Connecticut in play and the fact that he was the Democrat nominee for Vice President in 2000 would certainly create a lot of buzz. It would definitely be an interesting selection.*

bare when it comes to potential Vice Presidential nominees who provide ethnic and/or gender diversity and who also have requisite experience in the political arena.

The first pool of female prospects will come from the Senatorial or Gubernatorial ranks. There are a number of women Republican U.S. Senators who could make the list for consideration, but some are too liberal to be embraced by the party faithful (Senators Susan Collins and Olympia Snow, both of Maine) or come from states that should be firmly in the Republican column anyway (Senator Elizabeth Dole of North Carolina and Senator Kay Bailey Hutchison of Texas). Connecticut Governor Jodi Rell will get some attention, but she is even more liberal than Collins and Snow.

The Thompson team could turn to the U.S. House for additional female prospects. However, there seems to be a pretty strong historical bias against those in that body when it comes to the selection of Vice Presidential candidates.[175]

The list of potential "minority" contenders within the Republican Party may be even shorter than the list of viable women. In the Senate there is Senator Mel Martinez of Florida, who would have appeal among Hispanic voters. As a former Secretary of Housing and Urban Development under President George W. Bush, he has some administrative experience that other candidates lack. However, he was born in Cuba and is therefore barred by the U.S. Constitution from seeking the position.[176]

Some other Bush Cabinet members might make good choices for a Thompson Vice President except for running afoul of this same provision of the Constitution. Commerce Secretary Carlos Gutierrez, who was previously CEO of the

---

175 *In fact the last House member to be elected Vice President was John Nance Garner (the man who described the job as "not worth a bucket of warm spit") who served under President Franklin Delano Roosevelt from 1933-1941. Nance had run a tough race against FDR for the top spot before negotiating for the VP slot.*

176 *Article 2, Section 1, Clause 5 specifies that the President and Vice President must be "natural born" citizens of the United States.*

Kellogg Company, is another prospect who is disqualified because he was born in Cuba. Labor Secretary Elaine Chao was born in Taiwan.[177]

As he looks beyond the Senate for other choices, Thompson will probably take a strong look at former Maryland Lt. Governor Michael Steele, an African American who lost a hotly contested and high profile race for the U.S. Senate in 2006. Another African American who will get consideration is former Ohio Secretary of State Ken Blackwell, who was also formerly Mayor of Cincinnati. Ohio is a critical state, and the question is whether he would help carry that state despite being soundly defeated in the Governor's race there in 2006. Had either of these two men been successful in their 2006 campaigns it might have been impossible to keep them OFF the ticket in 2008, but both failed to win.

Others who will almost certainly receive consideration will include former Oklahoma Congressman J.C. Watts, who has brilliant star power among Republican conservatives, but may not be able to draw black Democrats across the aisle. Herman Cain, the former CEO of Godfather's Pizza, who is now a syndicated columnist and radio talk host, will generate some talk as well. Cain recently survived a bout with colon cancer and that might make the Thompson team shy away from him. He ran for the Republican nomination for the U.S. Senate in Georgia in 2004, losing to eventual winner Senator Johnny Isakson.

Eventually, following countless meetings, mind-numbing reviews of lists, polling data and analysis, and after talking to experts and grassroots supporters across the country, the focus for a Republican nominee for Vice President in 2008 may come back to a name that generated speculation from the outset: Condoleezza Rice.

---

177 *California Governor Arnold Schwarzenegger is another who is excluded from consideration because he was born in Austria.*

CONDOLEEZZA RICE

Condoleezza Rice is the 66th Secretary of State for the United States. She is the first African American woman to serve in that position.[178] But "who she is", and how she became one of the most powerful women in the world, is more important than the position she currently holds.[179] While her gender and ethnicity would make her an asset as a Vice Presidential nominee with Fred Thompson (or any other Republican nominee), her extraordinary competence, personal story, and intellect are even more important qualifications.[180]

Condi Rice is the great-great granddaughter of slaves. But by the time she was born there were three generations of college-educated family members, including teachers, preachers and lawyers. Her father John Rice was a Presbyterian minister and teacher. Her mother Angelena, who was a science and music teacher, crafted her name from the Italian musical notation "*con dolcezza*" (with sweetness). She soon became simply, "Condi".

She was raised in Titusville, Alabama, one of Birmingham's black middle-class neighborhoods, where many of the harsh realities of racial segregation that gripped the city were kept at bay. But the segregation that divided Birmingham and the rest of the nation could not be ignored, even by a little girl with a family that kept her away from the places she was most likely to be confronted with the bigotry of the times.

Rice has recounted instances when she personally suffered discrimination because of race: being relegated to a storage room at a department store instead of a regular dressing room, being barred from going to the circus or the local amusement

---

178 *Madeleine Albright was the first woman; Colin Powell the first African American.*
179 *In 2004 and 2005 she was ranked as the most powerful woman in the world by Forbes magazine; she was second to newly elected German Chancellor Angela Merkel in 2006. In 2007 Time named her among the 100 Most Influential in the World.*
180 *Dick Morris and Eileen McGann brilliantly detailed the qualifications that Condi Rice has to be President (and the reasons why Republicans should nominate her in 2008 to defeat Hillary Clinton) in their 2006 book "Condi vs. Hillary." All of the reasons*

park, being denied hotel rooms, and even being given bad food at restaurants. Rice has said of that time: "Those terrible events burned into my consciousness. I missed many days at my segregated school because of the frequent bomb threats."[181]

Long before she took a lead role in the global "War on Terror," Rice felt the effects of terrorism herself. She was only eight years old when her schoolmate Denise McNair, aged 11, was killed by white supremacists who bombed the primarily African American Sixteenth Street Baptist Church on September 15, 1963. The events of that day and the days that followed clearly shaped her world view, and it has helped her shape history.

On May 13, 2004 Rice gave the Commencement Address at Vanderbilt University in Nashville, Tennessee. She noted how the events of that tragic day in 1963 provide lessons for us today:

> "I remember the bombing of that Sunday School at 16th Street Baptist Church in Birmingham in 1963. I did not see it happen, but I heard it happen, and I felt it happen, just a few blocks away at my father's church. It is a sound that I will never forget, that will forever reverberate in my ears. That bomb took the lives of 4 young girls, including my friend and playmate, Denise McNair. The crime was calculated, not random. It was meant to suck the hope out of young lives, bury their aspirations and ensure that all fears would be propelled forward into the next generation. But those fears were not propelled forward, those terrorists failed. They failed because of the poverty of their vision, a vision of hate and inequality and the primacy of difference, and they failed because of the courage and sacrifice of all who suffered and struggled for civil rights. Those brave men and women asked America to make a choice between living up to our founding ideas, or perpetuating State sanctioned

181 Antonia Felix, "Condi: The Condoleezza Rice Story," Newmarket Press, 2d Edition (2005).

racism.

All people are bound together by several common desires. Never make the mistake of assuming that some people do not share your desire to live freely; to think and believe as you would like to see fit; to raise a family and educate children, boys and girls; never make the mistake of assuming that some people do not desire the freedom to chart their own course in life. In my professional life I have listened as some explained why Russians would never embrace freedom, that military dictatorship would always be a way of life in Latin America, that Asian values were incompatible with democracy and that tyranny, corruption and one-party rule would always dominate Africa.

Today we hear these same doubts about possibility of freedom in the Middle East. We have to reject those doubts. Knowing what we know about the difficulties of our own history, knowing the history of Alabama and Mississippi and Tennessee, we should be humble in singing freedom's praise, but our voice should never waver in speaking out on the side of those who seek freedom, and we should never indulge in the condescending voices that allege that some people are not interested in freedom, or aren't ready for freedom's responsibility. That view was wrong in 1963 in Birmingham, and it's wrong in 2004 in Baghdad."[182]

The girl who still remembers the small coffins that buried her schoolmates went on to graduate at age 19 from the University of Denver with a degree in political science. She picked up a Masters Degree (political science) from Notre Dame and in 1981, earned her PhD at the Graduate School of International Studies at the University of Denver. Along the way she became extraordinarily proficient in the piano and learned to speak Russian, German, French and Spanish.

In 1981 she was hired as an Assistant Professor at Stanford

182 Condoleezza Rice, Commencement Address, Vanderbilt University, May 13, 2004.

University. Six years later she was granted tenure and promoted to Associate Professor. In 1993, she became the first female, first minority and youngest Provost in Stanford history.[183]

As Provost, Rice was responsible for managing the university's multi-billion dollar budget. It may have given us a glimpse of her budget cutting skills. At the time she took the post, Stanford was running a deficit of $20 million. She promised that the budget deficit would be balanced within "two years." Coit Blacker, who was Stanford's deputy director of the Institute for International Studies, said there "was a sort of conventional wisdom that said it couldn't be done ... that [the deficit] was structural, that we just had to live with it."[184] Two years later, Rice announced that the deficit been eliminated and the university was holding a record surplus of over $14.5 million.

On December 17, 2000, Rice was named by President-elect George W. Bush as National Security Advisor, the first female to hold that position. When Colin Powell stepped down as Secretary of State, Bush named Rice to fill that important office.

Like most people, Condoleezza Rice is more than a series of accomplishments and job titles. While millions of Americans recognize her name and face, they are most likely totally unfamiliar with her in terms of her personal motivations and character. It is impossible to have any appreciation of who she is without recognizing the importance that she places on her religious faith.

> "My faith is a part of everything that I do," she has said. "It's not something that I can set outside of anything that I do, because it's so integral to who I am. And prayer is very important to me and a belief that if you ask for it, you will be guided. Now, that doesn't mean that I think

183 The Provost is the chief budget and academic officer of the University. Rice served as Provost from 1993-2000.
184 James Robinson, "Velvet-Glove Forcefulness", Stanford Report Online, June 9, 1999.

*that God will tell me what to do on, you know, the Iran
nuclear problem. That's not how I see it. But I do believe
very strongly that if you are a prayerful and faithful
person, that that is a help in guiding us, as imperfect
beings, to have to deal with extremely difficult and
consequential matters."*[185]

Because of her central role in the response to the terror
attack of 9-11, the War in Afghanistan and the War in Iraq,
Rice will definitely be the target of criticism in any campaign.
But that will be true of anybody who runs for President or Vice
President, and she is more than up to the task of taking the
heat. She is not a staunch conservative on some issues
important to the Republican base. For example, she describes
herself as "mildly pro-choice" while supporting restrictions on
federal funding of abortion, a ban on late-term abortions, and a
requirement of parental notification.[186]

However, Rice is a strong proponent of the Second
Amendment and is certainly "hawkish" enough on foreign policy
to satisfy even the strongest pro-America conservative. Her
approval ratings in opinion polls have remained consistently
high, despite the low ratings received by President Bush and his
Administration.[187] Those ratings are likely to improve as voters
actually get to know her and her incredible story.

As Secretary of State, Rice has logged millions of miles
traveling the world and engaging in personal diplomacy. The
skills she has honed in that effort would pay huge dividends if
she were to be just as dogged in traveling throughout the
United States as a candidate for Vice President. Based upon her
track record of discipline, perseverance, focus and success
throughout her life, it is hard to imagine that she would pursue
a political campaign any differently.

---

185 *Bill Sammon, "2008 Run, Abortion Engage Her Politically," Washington Times, March
12, 2005. www.washtimes.com/national/20050311-115948-2015r.htm*
186 *Id.*
187 *For example, a Fox News/Opinion Dynamics poll of 900 registered voters conducted
April 18-19, 2006 gave Condi Rice a 60% approval rating, with an 86% approval rating
among Republicans.*

WHAT ABOUT COLIN POWELL?

A few years ago General Colin Powell would have been considered an essential part of any Republican presidential "Dream Team." The retired Chairman of the Joint Chiefs of Staff (the first African American to hold that position) and former Secretary of State (again, the first African American to serve) has certainly seen his luster damaged by the intelligence failures that led to overstated claims of weapons of mass destruction being in the possession of Iraqi dictator Saddam Hussein. The fact that Powell was actually more skeptical about the basis for and imminent need for action against Hussein has not shielded him from criticism for his role in the decision-making that led to the Iraq War.

Yet, he still retains remarkable credibility, has a commanding presence that would enable him to stand side by side with Fred Thompson and convey comparable strength and ability. At a time when the threat of terror on the scale of 9-11 or worse remains a very real possibility, it would be a ticket that could give America comfort in knowing "they" are in charge. It could properly be called a "Dream Team."

The selection of Powell by Thompson would certainly spur some criticism from conservatives. Powell is pro-choice on the issue of abortion, has supported "reasonable" gun control and affirmative action. If he was seeking the top spot on the ticket those issues would prove troublesome. But having a solid conservative like Thompson as the presidential nominee would serve to deflect that criticism. Republicans would also be highly motivated to find a ticket that could counter some of the gender and ethnic advantages that the Democrats would enjoy: so, overlooking a soft spot or two on issues would be something that they could swallow.

Would Powell accept the Vice Presidential spot if it was offered? He would not be inclined to take the political plunge with just anybody, but he has had a positive relationship with Fred Thompson and their styles of leadership would blend well together. There is also the Howard Baker connection that could come into play. When Powell was Ronald Reagan's National Security Advisor, former Majority Leader Baker was serving as White House Chief of Staff. The two men got along very well, and he was considered to be another of Baker's political protégés — just like Fred Thompson.

Longtime House Speaker Thomas "Tip" O'Neill used to declare that "all politics is local." It is also personal. That personal connection with Baker and Thompson just could be the link that lures Powell into the political arena in 2008.

THE BIG TWELVE

No matter who the Republican and Democratic Party nominees are in 2008, and regardless of who those nominees select to fill out the ticket, the 2008 Presidential campaign most likely hinges on the results in twelve key states. Some of these states will become more or less significant as political steps and missteps are made during the course of the campaign; and a few others may enter the mix. If a Vice Presidential selection shuffles the deck, or a terror attack changes the political dynamic in one or more states, or if a candidate makes a major mistake that suddenly puts a "safe" state in play, then the "Big Twelve" could change... but only slightly.

For the most part, more money will be spent and more campaign resources will be deployed to "The Big Twelve" because they are the ones that can be properly characterized as "swing states." They almost certainly will determine who wins and who loses in 2008. Fred Thompson has strengths that will play particularly well in each of these critical states, underscoring the significance of the "Fred Factor" in 2008.

Three of these states have been close enough to swing from one party to the other between 2000 and 2004. Iowa and New Mexico were narrowly carried by Gore over Bush in 2000; but in 2004, Bush moved the two states into the Republican column by edging Kerry. New Hampshire was closely won by Bush in 2000, but Kerry carried the day in 2004. All three will be up for grabs in 2008.

Another key state, Wisconsin, has seen less than half point victory margins for the Democrats in both of the last two elections. It will most certainly be bitterly contested again in 2008.

Four other states that comprise "The Big Twelve" were among the top ten states with the closest margin in both 2000 AND 2004: Oregon, Minnesota, Ohio, and Nevada. And the final four, Pennsylvania, Michigan, Florida and Missouri ranked among the tightest margins in EITHER 2000 or 2004.

The remaining thirty eight states have been fairly consistent in their presidential voting patterns in the past two election cycles. Ultimately, politics is a local game, but the global impact of the Presidential contest in 2008 – both in terms of international events having an effect on the race and the race having an effect on international events – will nationalize the race more than ever before. The close divide between Red State-Blue State America and the partisan gulf between Right and Left also magnifies and intensifies every right and wrong move that the candidates make. All of those aspects of the political atmosphere in 2008 will be on full display with the bright lights of scrutiny glaring in the Big Twelve states that will determine who wins the White House.

STATES WITH SMALLEST MARGIN OF VICTORY, 2000.

	State	Total Vote	% Margin	Margin	*Gore*	**Bush**	Nader
1	**FL**	5,963,110	**0.01%**	**537**	48.84%	**48.85%**	1.63%
2	*NM*	598,605	0.06%	366	47.91%	**47.85%**	3.55%
3	*WI*	2,598,607	0.22%	5,708	47.83%	**47.61%**	3.62%
4	*IA*	1,315,563	0.31%	4,144	48.54%	**48.22%**	2.23%
5	*OR*	1,533,968	0.44%	6,765	46.96%	**46.52%**	5.04%
6	**NH**	569,081	**1.27%**	**7,211**	46.80%	48.07%	3.90%
7	*MN*	2,438,685	2.40%	58,607	47.91%	**45.50%**	5.20%
8	**MO**	2,359,892	**3.34%**	**78,786**	47.08%	**50.42%**	1.63%
9	**OH**	4,705,457	**3.51%**	**165,019**	46.46%	**49.97%**	2.50%
10	**NV**	608,970	**3.55%**	**21,597**	45.98%	**49.52%**	2.46%

Source: 2000 Presidential Election Results, www.uselectionatlas.org

STATES WITH SMALLEST MARGIN OF VICTORY, 2004.

State		Total Vote	% Margin	Margin	**Bush**	*Kerry*	Other
1	*WI*	2,997,007	*0.38%*	*11,384*	**49.32%**	*49.70%*	0.98%
2	**IA**	1,506,908	**0.67%**	**10,059**	**49.90%**	*49.23%*	0.87%
3	**NM**	756,304	**0.79%**	**5,988**	**49.84%**	*49.05%*	1.11%
4	*NH*	677,738	*1.37%*	*9,274*	**48.87%**	*50.24%*	0.88%
5	**OH**	5,627,908	**2.11%**	**118,601**	**50.81%**	*48.71%*	0.48%
6	*PA*	5,769,590	*2.50%*	*144,248*	**48.42%**	*50.92%*	0.65%
7	**NV**	829,587	**2.59%**	**21,500**	**50.47%**	*47.88%*	1.65%
8	*MI*	4,839,252	*3.42%*	*165,437*	**47.81%**	*51.23%*	0.96%
9	*MN*	2,828,387	*3.48%*	*98,319*	**47.61%**	*51.09%*	1.30%
10	*OR*	1,836,782	*4.16%*	*76,332*	**47.19%**	*51.35%*	1.46%

Source: 2004 Presidential Election Results,
www.uselectionatlas.org

IOWA

I n the past two Presidential election cycles no state has reflected the narrow divide between victory and defeat better than the State of Iowa. In 2000, Gore carried the state and its 7 Electoral Votes by the miniscule margin of .31% by winning just 4,144 votes more than Bush. In 2004, the state's Electoral Votes ended up in the Bush column. Bush won by 10,059 votes — a winning edge of just .67%, a veritable landslide by Iowa standards! How will this "swing" state turn in 2008?[188]

The political "split personality" of Iowa is further reflected by the fact that the state's two U.S. Senators are Republican Senator Charles Grassley and Democrat Senator Tom Harkin. Harkin is up for re-election in 2008, and in a state that is so narrowly divided politically, his presence on the ballot could be a factor in the presidential results.

One of the early decisions that Fred Thompson will face if he enters the race is whether he can assemble the organization and grass roots leadership to compete in the Iowa Straw Poll in August, 2007. The bigger question will be whether he chooses to compete in the Iowa Caucuses in January.

Candidates like Romney, McCain and others have been setting up neighborhood level grass-roots support in Iowa for about a year. Some of those who have chosen other candidates would likely jump ship and join the Thompson campaign, but are there enough voters up for grabs or willing to change teams at this point to accomplish what is necessary to win in Iowa? As noted earlier, Thompson can gauge support in Iowa and make a decision about the Straw Poll as late as a few days before it takes place. Giuliani may also skip that Straw Poll which would give Thompson an easy out, or big opportunity to further close the gap with Rudy by getting a big win or top-tier finish just weeks after getting in the race.

---

188 *For timely updates on updated political news in Iowa, go to www.iowapolitics.com.*

But the Caucuses are more problematic. Skipping them will definitely give the Mainstream Media something to talk about. Other candidates will add fuel to the fire. And, despite the fact that John McCain skipped both the Straw Poll and the Caucuses in 2000, he did not have to ultimately come back to the state and seek their votes in the general election. Iowa has been so closely contested in the "real" election the past few cycles that the decision of whether or not to participate in the Caucuses may carry over into the general election itself.

For Thompson, skipping the Iowa Caucuses might make sense from the standpoint of "primary" politics, but that could come back to haunt him later.

A late entry into the Presidential race will not have much impact on Thompson's chances overall, but in Iowa and New Hampshire a late start has implications beyond the primary process. Because of that, Thompson faces the daunting challenge of organizing a grassroots campaign while others are way ahead of him and while there are few bodies remaining to be recruited. None of this would matter much if the 11 Electoral College votes represented collectively by Iowa and New Hampshire did not loom quite so large in what may be a very, very close contest.

NEW MEXICO

Another state that flipped to the Republican column from the Democrat column between 2000 and 2004 is New Mexico. In 2000, Gore carried the state by a margin of just 366 votes (.06%). But in 2004, Bush won over Kerry by 5,988 votes (.79%).

Like Iowa, the state's two U.S. Senators come from each side of the aisle. Republican Senator Pete Domenici is up for re-election in 2008 while, Democrat Jeff Bingaman is safe until 2012. Popular Governor Bill Richardson is running for the Democrat nomination for President, and his presence on the ticket (most likely as a Vice Presidential nominee) could have a huge impact on where the state's 5 Electoral Votes end up.

In recent years, the growing Hispanic population in the state has steadily moved it in the Democrat direction, but the state is still fundamentally conservative. New Mexico Congresswoman Heather Wilson (and to a lesser extent Senator Domenici) was embroiled in the controversial firing of U.S. Attorney David Iglesias. Iglesias was outspoken in his criticism of his removal, which led to the investigation of the role of Attorney General Alberto Gonzales in that process, but it appears unlikely that the dispute will have any significant impact on the 2008 election.

Domenici being on the ballot in 2008 could help to bring the Republicans in the state out of their disarray, which would dramatically improve the prospects of a victory in the Presidential race. But if the ticket is Hillary-Richardson, the Republicans may be forced to get the 5 Electoral Votes represented by New Mexico somewhere else.

NEW HAMPSHIRE

While Iowa and New Mexico shifted from the Democrat column to the Republican column between 2000 and 2004, one state went the other way. Bush carried the Granite State in 2000 by 7,211 votes (a margin of 1.27%). Kerry was able to bag the state's four Electoral Votes in 2004 when turnout increased by over 100,000 votes, a jump of nearly 19%. Kerry won by 9,274 votes (1.37%).

New Hampshire used to be a reliable Republican haven in a sea of Northeastern Democrat states, but that has changed in the past two decades. A Democrat Governor, John Lynch, is in a second term, and Republican Senator John Sununu will likely face a tough bid for reelection in 2008 in a state that continues to trend in a more liberal direction. An example of the trend is the fact that the state recently became the fourth state to legalize civil unions for gays and lesbians. Even the mention of supporting higher taxes used to be the kiss of political death in New Hampshire, but Governor Lynch has been confident enough of his own hold on power to allow talk of imposing a new state income tax on residents of New Hampshire and has emerged unscathed, so far.

Like those in Iowa, New Hampshire voters expect to see a lot of a presidential candidate before they give their vote. The compressed calendar of primaries that come on the heels of the nation's first primary election in New Hampshire will tempt some candidates to ration their time in the Granite State, but they will risk losing votes by doing so. Fred Thompson's charisma and plain talk on the issues that matter to voters in New Hampshire will be helpful, but he will still have to spend time in the state to get the votes…both in the primary and the general election. As is the case in Iowa, giving New Hampshire short shrift during the primary may make sense, except for its importance in November, 2008.

WISCONSIN

W hile a few states have shifted back and forth between Republicans and Democrats in the last two election cycles, Wisconsin has remained in the Democrat column… but only by the narrowest of margins. In 2000, Gore carried the state by only 5,708 votes out of over two and a half million! That .22% margin in 2000 gave Gore the state's eleven Electoral Votes that year

Nearly 3 million people voted in the 2004 presidential race in Wisconsin, and the state had one less Electoral Vote. But the gap between the two parties was tight again. Kerry prevailed by .38% — just 11,384 votes.

In 2008, the focus of the state's politics will be on the presidential campaign since there are no statewide races slated for Wisconsin.[189] Thompson's "Reaganesque" qualities will certainly be attractive to the blue collar Reagan Democrats in the state that gave Ronald Reagan large margins of victory in 1980 and 1984.[190]

OREGON

Oregon is another state that was carried easily by Ronald Reagan in 1980 and 1984, but where Republican presidential fortunes have suffered miserably ever since. George W. Bush did narrow the gap considerably in 2000, losing to Al Gore by a margin of only .44%. However, the 5% of the vote garnered by third party candidate Ralph Nader (who picked up 77,000 votes in Oregon) was a big factor in making that contest close. In 2004, John Kerry won the state by a little over 4%.

Oregon has consistently been in the Democrat column in recent years, but depending on the presence of third party candidates, the contentious nature of the Democrat primary battle, the potential "star power" of the Republican ticket and events unforeseen at this point, it could be in play for 2008.

OHIO

Ohio was once a reliable bastion of Republican support, but Republican leadership within the state has been a disaster in the past decade. Republican Governor Robert Taft ran for a second term as Governor in 2002 promising voters that he would oppose any new tax hikes. However, with the help of a Republican legislature, he quickly pushed through a multi-billion dollar tax increase as he began his second term. The "low tax, small government" Republican

---

189 *For updates on Wisconsin politics go to www.wispolitics.com.*
190 *President George H. W. Bush lost the state to Michael Dukakis in 1988 by a margin of 51.4% to 47.8%.*

base in the state became increasingly disaffected with the Governor and their own party. When Taft was later convicted on misdemeanor charges for violating state ethics rules governing gifts and other benefits, his approval ratings plummeted to a low of 6.7% in November, 2005.[191]

Republican fortunes in the state took another hit when popular Congressman Bob Ney was implicated in bribery and corruption charges in May, 2006. Ney chose not to seek re-election and on October 13, 2006, he pled guilty to charges of conspiracy and making false statements in connection with the Jack Abramoff Indian Casino lobbying scandal.[192]

Against this backdrop of disarray, the 2006 election cycle saw Republicans lose the state's U.S. Senate seat held by incumbent Mike Dewine to Democrat Congressman Sherrod Brown, along with Ney's seat in the House.

In the 2000 Presidential election, Ohio ended up in the Bush column by a margin of 3.5%. Against Kerry in 2004, Bush carried the state by 2.11%. If Republicans in Ohio can heal the divisive fractures that have developed over the past decade, then Ohio and its crucial twenty Electoral Votes could be a relatively secure state in the 2008 Presidential campaign.

MINNESOTA

On April 14, 2007 an estimated 7,000 Minnesotans gathered on the steps of the State Capitol in St. Paul to protest in favor of tax relief.[193] The purpose of the rally was to deliver signatures from over 18,000 taxpayers gathered on talk station KTLK's Web site in opposition to new taxes that were being proposed in the State Legislature. The left-wing Democrat Farm Labor Party, with majorities in the State House

---

191 Jim Tankersly, "*Taft's Approval Ratings Sink Into Single Digits,*" *Toledo Blade,* November 29, 2005.
192 *On January 19, 2007 Ney was sentenced to thirty months in prison.*
193 Jason Lewis, "*Land of 10,000 Taxes,*" *Wall Street Journal,* April 16, 2007.

and Senate, was pushing a dizzying array of new taxes totaling $4 billion in a state with five million people and a biennial state budget of $31.5 billion.[194] If taxpayers in Minnesota stay revved up through the 2008 election, it could give Republicans a chance to move the state into the Republican column in the presidential race.

Al Gore carried Minnesota over George W. Bush in the 2000 election by a 2.4% margin. (Ralph Nader received 5.2% of the total vote.) John Kerry captured the state's ten Electoral Votes in 2004, winning 51.09% to 47.61%.

In 2008 Republican Senator Norm Coleman faces reelection against a field of potential Democrat Farm Labor nominees that includes comedian and liberal talk host Al Franken. Coleman is seen as vulnerable by many national political experts, although few believe Franken will emerge as the Democrat nominee.

Nevertheless, strange things do happen in Minnesota politics. In 1998, former professional wrestler Jesse Ventura was elected Governor, beating Coleman (who was then Mayor of St. Paul) and Democrat Farm Labor nominee Hubert "Skip" Humphrey, III (who was State Attorney General.)[195] Ventura's main campaign promise which led him to victory was to "cut taxes."

NEVADA

Nevada would seem to be a dependable part of "red state" America, although Bill Clinton carried it twice. Bush carried the state in both 2000 (by 3.55%) and 2004 (by 2.59%), each time by about 21,000 votes. The state's population is growing rapidly, with many transplants from California fueling that growth. Despite its Republican leanings over the years, Nevada is probably more Libertarian in its views

---

194 Id.
195 *Ventura achieved approval ratings in the 73% range early in his term, but did not seek a second term. He now lives in Baja California, Mexico.*

than Republican. It is, after all, a state where both gambling and prostitution are legal.

The state has a Democrat Senator (Majority Leader Harry Reid) and a Republican Senator (John Ensign); neither of them is on the ballot in 2008. Reid's higher profile as Majority Leader may have an impact on his re-election prospects in 2010, as his efforts to please the more liberal national Democratic Party establishment puts him at ideological odds with more conservative Nevada voters. That profile could play a role in where the state's five Electoral votes end up in 2008.

PENNSYLVANIA

Twenty-one Electoral Votes are up for grabs in Pennsylvania in 2008, tying it with Illinois as the fifth biggest prize. Republicans need to make a strong bid to move the Keystone State from blue to red to win the White House. In 2004, Kerry beat Bush 50.92% to 48.43% in a state that Republicans had targeted early on. Pennsylvania has gone with the winner in eight of the last ten presidential contests.

Neither of the two U.S. Senators (Republican Arlen Specter and Democrat Bob Casey, Jr.) will be on the ballot in 2008. Democrat Governor Ed Rendell won reelection in 2006, so the Governor's office is also secure for 2008. There are three of the State's Constitutional Officers who will face elections in 2008, but most of the focus will be on the Presidential race.

Fred Thompson could make a strong play for the hearts, minds and votes of Pennsylvanians by relying on the Reaganesque qualities that enabled Ronald Reagan to win the state in both 1980 and 1984.

MICHIGAN

Michigan has been caught up in a bitter budget battle throughout 2007 as Democrat Governor Jennifer Granholm and the Legislature have fought over how to deal with a billion dollar budget shortfall. Tax increases, layoffs and draconian cuts have all been on the table at one point during the "negotiations" that have frequently ended up in name-calling sessions. That budget crisis, along with the continued evacuation of jobs from Michigan and fears over the impact of tougher environmental restrictions on the state's automobile industry may place it firmly in the "swing state" category in 2008. With seventeen Electoral Votes, it is certainly a desirable target for both Democrats and Republicans.

In 2004, George W. Bush had high hopes for the state and visited often. But at the end of the day, Kerry won by a 51.23% to 47.81% spread. Reagan carried the state handily in both 1980 and 1984; Clinton did the same in 1992 and 1996.

Mitt Romney was born in the state (in Detroit) and could argue "favorite son" status with voters if he secures the Republican nomination. However, Fred Thompson has more stylistic and ideological connections with the blue collar Reagan Democrats who will decide where Michigan lands in 2008. If he was to trot out the big red Chevy pickup truck on the campaign trail, Michigan might be the right place.

FLORIDA

There are close election margins. There are razor-thin election margins. And then, there is Florida, 2000. The .01% margin of victory for George W. Bush captivated a nation for weeks as "hanging chads" were examined under microscopic scrutiny from partisan activists on both sides. There was every expectation that Florida 2004 would be a repeat of the drama. But Bush carried the state by a fairly significant margin and attention turned elsewhere.

In 2008, all eyes could be back on Florida, particularly if the Democrat ticket is Hillary-Richardson and the Sunshine State's large Latino-Hispanic population is fully energized at the prospect of the first Hispanic on a national ticket. None of the state's major political offices are up for grabs in 2008, so all the attention will be on presidential politics. Twenty seven Electoral Votes go to the winner, with only California, Texas and New York carrying more weight. Florida is a prize worth fighting for, and the nominees will spend a lot of time soliciting the attention of the state's voters.

MISSOURI

With eleven Electoral Votes, Missouri ranks as another important "swing state" that will be worth an effort of resources in 2008. Bush won the state against Al Gore in by a modest margin of 3.34%. It was expected to be tightly contested again in 2004, but Bush stretched the margin against Kerry to a solid 7.2%.

Republican Governor Matt Blunt will be on the ballot for reelection in 2008.[196] Neither of the state's U.S. Senators, Republican Kit Bond and Democrat Claire McCaskill, will face voters in 2008.

Missouri is one of those states where candidates have to be successful in a wide variety of environments; from the urban centers of St. Louis and Kansas City, the wealthy suburbs surrounding those cities, and in the large rural expanses that make up the center of the state. Fred Thompson will be suited to appealing to those mid-America values, just as Ronald Reagan did a few decades ago.

---

196 *Blunt narrowly defeated Claire McCaskill in 2004. McCaskill then defeated incumbent Republican U.S. Senator Jim Talent in 2006, becoming the first woman elected to the U.S. Senate from Missouri in her own right.*

Fred on Capitol Hill

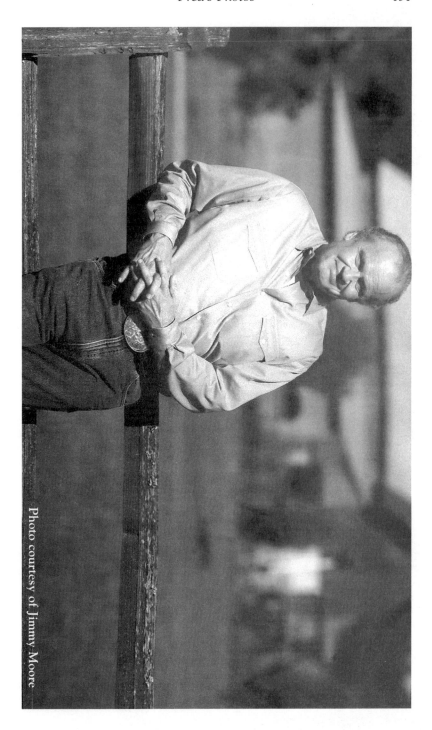

Photo courtesy of Jimmy Moore

Fred with Nancy Reagan, 1998

**Fred on his horse at Mule Day, 1994, Columbia, TN
Photo courtesy of Emily Booker**

Fred addressing the press outside the Capitol Hill Club,
April 18, 2007 with Congessman Zach Wamp

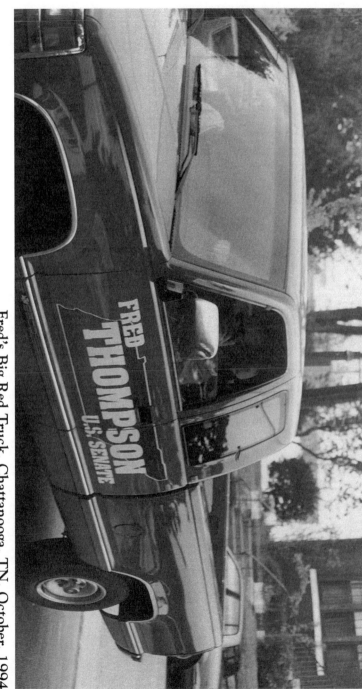

Fred's Big Red Truck, Chattanooga, TN, October, 1994
Photo courtesy of Dean Rice

Fred on the campaign trail with the Big Red Truck, October, 1996
Photo courtesy of Jimmy Moore

Fred on the campaign trail in the Big Red Truck bed, October, 1996
Photo courtesy of Jimmy Moore

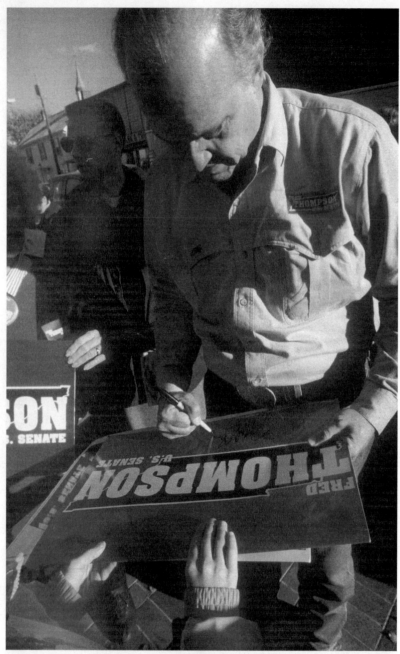

Fred on the campaign trail in November, 1996
Photo courtesy of Jimmy Moore

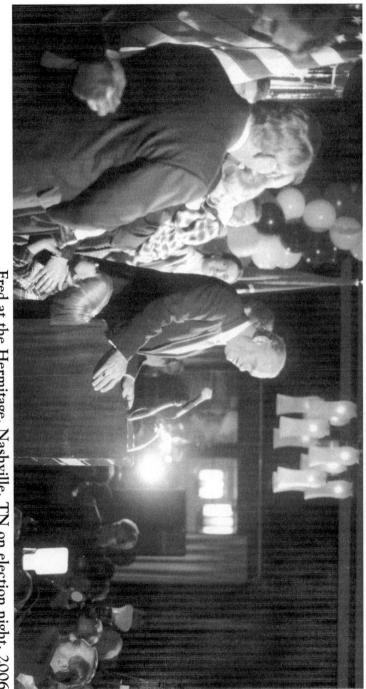

Fred at the Hermitage, Nashville, TN on election night, 2006
Photo courtesy of Jimmy Moore

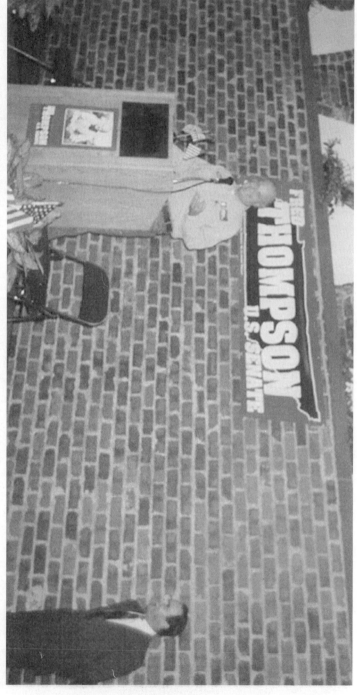

Congressman Fred Thompson with Congressman Zach Wamp in Chattanooga, TN, 2006
Photo courtesy of friends of Zach Wamp

Fred with Congressman Zach Wamp
at Wally's Restaurant, Chattanooga, TN, October, 1996
Photo courtesy of friends of Zach Wamp

Fred campaigning for Congressman Zach Wamp, 2006
Photo courtesy of friends of Zach Wamp

Section III: Where does Fred Stand?

C andidates for public office spend a lot of time talking about where they stand on the issues of the day. Many of them are masters at producing huge volumes of words… without ever really saying *anything* that could be considered a definitive statement. That is *not* how Fred Thompson speaks. That is not who he is.

From the moment he first indicated that he was "leaving the door open" to a potential race for President in a March 11, 2007 interview with Chris Wallace on "Fox News Sunday" he has been direct and open in talking about the issues, including the disclosure that he has a form of non-deadly lymphoma cancer. People in this country seem to be hungry for a leader who personifies straight talk, in both word and deed.

Why is Thompson considering a race for President? *"I think we're going into one of the most perilous times that our country has been in. I think that there are great opportunities out there. But it's not preordained that we're going to remain the strongest and freest nation in the history of the world. We've got to do some things well. We've got to do some things differently,"* Thompson told Wallace.[197]

On the issue of abortion Thompson was unequivocal: *"Pro-life."* Asked if he supported overturning *Roe v. Wade*, Thompson was equally unequivocal: *"I think Roe v. Wade was bad law and bad medical science And the way to address that is through good judges. I don't think the court ought to wake up one day and make new social policy for the country. It's contrary to what it's been the past 200 years… That's what happened in this case [Roe v. Wade]. I think it was wrong."*

---

197 *Transcript: http://www.foxnews.com/story/0,2933,258222,00.html*

What would Thompson do about Iraq?

"*I would do essentially what the president's doing. I know it's not popular right now, but I think we have to look down the road and consider the consequences of where we are.*

We're the leader of the free world whether we like it or not. People are looking to us to test our resolve and see what we're willing to do in resolving the situation that we have there. People think that if we hadn't gone down there, things would have been lovely.

If Saddam Hussein was still around today with his sons looking at Iran developing a nuclear capability, he undoubtedly would have reconstituted his nuclear capability. Things would be worse than what they are today.

We've got to rectify the mistakes that we've made. We went in there too light, wrong rules of engagement, wrong strategy, placed too much emphasis on just holding things in place while we built up the Iraqi army, took longer than we figured.

Wars are full of mistakes. You rectify things. I think we're doing that now. We're coming in with good people. We're coming in with a lot of different people. I know General Petraeus from when he was in Tennessee at Fort Campbell. He believes in the plan. He's convinced me that they can do the job.

Why would we not take any chance, even though there are certainly no guarantees, to not be run out of that place? I mean, we've got to take that opportunity and give it a chance to work."

In another later interview with Stephen F. Hayes of the *Weekly Standard*, Thompson would lay out a better explanation of the intelligence failures that preceded the military action against Saddam Hussein than the case put forward by the White House:

> "The irony here is that intelligence services had consistently over the years understated the capabilities of enemies and potential enemies. Now, here there was unanimity among the intelligence services, some of whom are supposed to be better than ours... People don't understand intelligence. They don't understand. It's seldom clear. It's often caveated. It's sometimes flat-out wrong. Different people often have different ideas. That's what a president is faced with. And some today would say that politically a president has got to have unanimity before he can make a choice. And then they say that if he has that unanimity, the president has to make that choice—at the same time talking about how deficient our capabilities are. But if those deficient capabilities produced a recommendation, the president of the United States and leader of the free world has to take that recommendation. That has been so faulty in the past. It's absurd. Presidents in the future, as always, have to make a determination based on a lot of things, and intelligence is one of them. And the president not only has the right to evaluate the intelligence that he's receiving, he has a duty to do that. He listens to the British. I mean, if history was any judge, I don't know about now, but if the Brits tell me that there's an [Iraqi] deal with Niger and our guys don't know whether there was or not, I tend to rely on the Brits. I mean, those are the calls the president's got to make, and the question is really: Which way do you want the president to lean? Caution –t hat it's probably not so? When bad news is delivered, he gets mixed messages, he gets various intelligence reports of various kinds. Did you want him all balled up in all of that, you know, trying to apply some kind of a scientific equation to it for fear that

> somebody in an intelligence committee is going to wave it
> around at a hearing later on or something like that? Is that
> what it's come to? If so, the world is going to be a lot more
> dangerous than it otherwise already is. You've got to
> exercise the authority and the responsibilities that you've
> been given. I mean, in this debate over intelligence and
> what it is and what it ought to be and how it's used and
> all of that, you know, [it] needs to be dealt with and laid
> out in a way that people can understand it. . . . The next
> report says somebody's got weapons of mass destruction,
> you know what're we going to do with that? You know,
> just because history—a cat won't sit on a hot stove twice,
> but he won't sit on a cold stove either."[198]

But perhaps the best response Fred Thompson gave during
the entire interview with Wallace was when confessed he did
not have all the answers when it came to ending American
dependence on foreign oil. Most Americans will find a political
candidate who does not know it all, or more importantly
doesn't think he does, to be remarkably refreshing. Yet, that is
Fred Thompson's "default setting."

If Thompson pursues the White House will he continue to
be so disarmingly straight in his responses to questions or will
he soon be captured by the "handlers," "wordsmiths," and
"pollsters" who typify modern campaigns? Will those who seek
to manage and nuance every moment keep Fred Thompson
from being Fred Thompson? His political success sprang forth
from the very moment he rejected the trappings and restraints
of a campaign *directed at* voters and relied on instead on his
unique skills to *communicate with* voters. It is unlikely that he
will forget that lesson.

In addition to his formidable skills as a communicator,
honed through years in front of the camera, Thompson also has
a record. At a time when many candidates may talk about what
they will do when it comes to the critical issues of the day,

---

198 Hayes, *"From the Courthouse…"*, *Weekly Standard*.

Thompson can point to a consistent record of actually voting like he talked. Others may *claim* to be conservative today, but Thompson has the *evidence* to back up his claims.

During his time in the Senate, national conservative groups gave Thompson consistently high marks for his voting record. Business groups gave him 90 to 100 point ratings; the Christian Coalition gave him a 92; the American Conservative Union gave him an 85. The National Taxpayers Union gave him an A rating. The National Rifle Association (NRA) has always been a firm supporter of Thompson.

Over the months and years ahead, many political experts and pundits will write volumes explaining what Fred thinks, where he stands, and what he means when it comes to particular issues. At the end of the day, however, Fred Thompson speaks with amazing clarity. He says what he means and means what he says. His words themselves are the best "Rosetta Stone" into the mind of Fred Thompson.

NATIONAL SECURITY AND THE WAR ON TERROR

Fred Thompson established a strong record on National Security and Defense issues during his career in the U.S. Senate, and he remained heavily involved in issues related to nuclear proliferation after he left the Senate. A speech he gave to the American Enterprise Institute on April 16, 2004 reveals his commitment to a strong response in the face of terror, as does his commentary in the wake of British sailors and marines being taken hostage by Iran in late March, 2007.

A NATION RESOLVED[199]

On September 20, 2001, President Bush spoke before a joint session of the United States Congress. It

---

[199] *Fred Thompson, speech to the American Enterprise Institute, Washington, D.C., April 16, 2004.*

had been nine days since the terrorist attacks in New York and Washington—a time when our nation displayed an extraordinary determination and strength. Americans understood the daunting task before us. We were a nation at war—and it would be a war, the President warned us, unlike any other we had fought before.

The President told us that this wasn't a war that would end with a great battle or the fall of an enemy capital. It wasn't another war to be won from 30,000 feet. And it wasn't going to be quick or easy.

As a member of the United States Senate, I joined my colleagues in applauding the President's blunt and honest outline of the battles ahead.

In the two and a half years since the President received a standing ovation from every member of the House and Senate, I have been flabbergasted at how quickly some have forgotten the words they applauded that day. Not only do these folks appear to have lost their spirit and determination, they have forgotten the spirit and determination of the American people.

The hand-wringing began early, just a few weeks after the September 11 attacks. When victory against the Taliban wasn't immediately forthcoming, they were out there talking about the "quagmire" in Afghanistan. We were in for a years-long fight, just like the Soviets before us. Days later, the Taliban collapsed.

In March of last year it was déjà vu all over again: Operation Iraqi Freedom was barely a week old when bad weather roused the prophets of defeat. We all remember them on the TV: The march to Baghdad had become hopelessly bogged down, they insisted. The invasion was going to be a humanitarian catastrophe, they warned. There would be countless casualties, both American and Iraqi.

In every war, the prophets of doom reach for the same old phrase book: Every significant battle facing the United States has been, and I quote, "another Vietnam."

But just as these voices were wrong in 1991, wrong in 2001, wrong in 2003, so too are they wrong again today.

Let's not minimize the challenges. Our nation faces a formidable enemy, in Iraq and elsewhere. Angry Baathists, fanatical Islamists and opportunistic terrorists from across the Middle East have perpetrated attacks against U.S. soldiers, U.S. allies, and against the Iraqi people themselves. Our resolve as a nation is being tested.

It's obvious we can't afford to cut and run. Even the most partisan critics admit as much. However, by invoking Vietnam, they are in effect predicting a U.S. defeat and pullout. Even as they give lip service to winning, they foment a sense of despair, instead of offering a strategy for victory.

Let's be blunt here: For many of President's critics there is a domestic constituency to be won from failure abroad. They are campaigning on defeat.

It's tempting to dismiss all of this as just another case of political opportunism. Plenty of cynics have learned to recognize the hand-wringing from Congress and elsewhere as nothing more than Washington electioneering.

But let's all step back a second and remember there's a nation of Americans and a world out there watching us. And these predictions of defeat have profound consequences in the real world. In every war, military historians will tell you, there is a strategic "center of gravity"—a tipping point that determines what direction *the larger conflict will go.*

The strategic center of gravity for this war is American willpower.

Our enemies know this. They know that they cannot defeat us in any conventional military contest, so instead, their aim is to demoralize us, to shake our resolve. They know that their only hope is in gruesome, made-for-television atrocities to undermine the confidence of the American public. Their purpose is not to win, but to convince us that we can't win, to break our will, to convince us to cut and run. Unfortunately, that strategy is not illogical. We have run before.

That and other past failures of will are among the main reasons we are under siege today.

Saddam Hussein invaded Kuwait in 1990 because he believed that Americans couldn't take casualties. He looked at Vietnam and Lebanon and concluded that the Americans didn't have the guts for a really tough fight.

After the war, when we took a pass on pushing to Baghdad, he concluded that he had been right all along. America's failure to confront Saddam during the 1990s, as he thwarted weapons inspectors and economic sanctions and corrupted the oil for food program, only spurred him further.

And unfortunately, Iraq wasn't the only time America's leaders have buckled under pressure.

In October 1983, the U.S. fled Lebanon after a suicide truck bombing killed 241 Marines in Beirut. We abandoned Somalia in 1993 after 18 U.S. soldiers were graphically murdered in a firefight with Islamic extremists, who, we later learned, were trained and funded by Osama Bin Laden's terrorist network.

In each case, while we avoided temporary difficulties, we became more vulnerable and our enemies grew stronger. Bin Laden boasted that Somalia proved America was a "paper tiger." Saddam concluded he could continue to flout the will of the international community, and that there wouldn't be any consequences. After the Clinton administration's muted response to first World Trade Center bombing in 1993; the bombings of our African embassies in August 1998; our non-response to the thwarted plot against Los Angeles International Airport during the millennium; as well as the October 2000 attack on the U.S.S. Cole—Al Qaeda thought we could be beat.

Undoubtedly our enemies were surprised after 9/11 when we turned out to be so much stronger than our record might otherwise suggest. Saddam seems to have persisted in the belief that we would not fight until the very moment American tanks appeared on the horizon.

Now, after Afghanistan and Iraq, no one should doubt the will of the American people; but the struggle in Iraq has given our enemies a new opportunity to test our will. They have scored some successes among our allies already, driving the Spanish to cut and run. They are trying, and failing, to do the same to Italy, Japan, South Korea and Poland. But where they have failed abroad, they have succeeded on our own shores: Every politician that describes Iraq as another Vietnam gives our enemies hope for success.

If we make this is another Vietnam, if we cut and run, we can count on the outcome: It will be a breeding ground for terrorism. Countries like Syria and Iran will be emboldened, convinced that they can harbor terrorists without threat of serious consequences.

If America were to reenact Vietnam, there would be

plenty of losers: Those in Iraq who had the courage to trust us will be cut down, just as they were in 1991. Those in Iraq who had the hope of finally living in freedom will be trampled, as will others in the Middle East eager to see a model of democracy in their region.

But the biggest loser of all would be the United States. We would be seen as an unsteady ally and a weak enemy. We would prove for once and for all that we don't have the courage to fight for the things we believe in, or to protect the long term interests of this country. Our enemies would believe that if our intelligence isn't 100 percent certain (and it never is); if we can't win every battle (and we never will), then we will not fight.

The truth is, the American people are better than that. They're stronger than that. The American people understand what's at stake here. And it's time that some of their leaders caught up with them.

The President's critics cannot have it both ways. They cannot claim to be in favor of winning the war in Iraq but also oppose fighting it, funding it, and offering any coherent strategy for succeeding at it. They cannot credibly claim to be in favor of winning the war while decrying it as a "mistake" that cannot be won.

And a coherent strategy for victory does not mean suggesting we escape our responsibilities in Iraq by turning them over to the United Nations or unnamed international allies. Our enemies recognize that this is a call to cut and run. And they are heartened by it.

Sure, there's a job to be done by the United Nations in Iraq, but that doesn't lessen our own obligation to defeat the terrorists and insurgents. And incidentally, for those who argue that the United Nations can bestow "legitimacy" on the occupation that the United States lacks, and that this will quell the insurgency, let me to remind you that insurgents bombed the UN mission to Iraq—twice.

Likewise, for those who argue that "internationalizing" the security force will allow us to win the war, I would simply ask what foreign nation should be in Iraq that is not already there. Does anyone seriously believe that the only thing keeping us from military victory in Iraq is a couple of platoons of French soldiers and a NATO stamp of approval?

The challenge of winning this fight is real and it is daunting. We should not confuse symbolic gestures for genuine strategy. Our enemies can tell the difference, and so should we.

The purpose of terrorism is to undermine public opinion here at home, to weaken the strategic center of gravity for this war. I believe, however, that the American center will hold. And when the President's political opponents run a campaign on defeat, it is they who will be defeated.

Contrary to the pronouncements of the prophets of defeat, Americans don't walk away from a challenge. And we're not going to run away from this fight. In September 2001 we became a nation filled with resolve; I believe we still are.

PIRATES OF TEHRAN[200]

Oil prices fell. The stock market rose. Video images of smiling British soldiers with Iranian President Ahmadinejad were everywhere. So were pictures of the

200 Fred Thompson blog post, April 8, 2007 at www.redstate.com.

15 freed hostages embracing family members back home. The relief over the return of the Brits was so tremendous; you could almost hear birds singing.

Maybe it's because military action won't be needed or maybe it's just because the ordeal won't drag on and on, but the world is breathing easier now. A lot of folks are happy. The problem, as I see it, is that Ahmadinejad seems to be the happiest.

And why shouldn't he be? He has shown the world that his forces can kidnap British citizens, subject them to brutal psychological tactics to coerce phony confessions, finagle the release of a high-ranking Iranian terror coordinator in Iraq, utterly trash the Geneva conventions and suffer absolutely no consequences.

The UN Security Council summoned its vaunted multilateral greatness to issue a swift statement of sincere uneasiness. The EU, which has pressured Britain to rely on Europeans for mutual defense instead of the U.S., wouldn't even discuss economic sanctions that might disrupt their holidays. Even NATO was AWOL.

Tony Blair doesn't appear to be in much of a mood for celebrating. I don't know how he could be, given the troubling spectacle of British soldiers shaking the hand of their kidnapper as a condition of release. In the old days, they would have kissed his ring — but wearing Iranian suits and carrying swag more appropriate to a Hollywood awards ceremony may have been as embarrassing. Ironically, Blair's options are fewer by the day as his own party moves to mothball the British fleet, once the fear of pirates and tyrants the world over.

Some in the West seem part of Iran's propaganda war; claiming that the release of the hostages was a victory that proves the Iranian dictatorship can be reasoned with. To misrepresent unpunished piracy as a victory is as Orwellian as the congressional mandate banning use of the term "the global war on terror." What are we — Reuters?

Ahmadinejad must be particularly pleased to see "deep thinking" journalists making the case that American actions in Iraq were the true cause of the kidnappings. To believe this, all you have to do is ignore the history of the Iranian Revolution, which has been in the extortion business ever since it took power. Between the 1979 American embassy crisis in Tehran and the seizure of Israeli soldiers last year by Iran's Hezbollah proxies, there have been more than a hundred other examples.

If you include the imprisonment of pro-Democracy dissidents and non-Shi'a Muslim minorities within Iran, the number reaches easily into the tens of thousands. The dwindling and persecuted Christian population of Iran, I suspect, found little joy in Ahmadinejad's explanation that he was freeing his victims as an "Easter gift."

It is critical that we see this incident as part of a long pattern of behavior — that will continue as long as the current leadership is in power. More importantly, it will escalate unimaginably if Iran achieves nuclear status, and with it the ability to hold millions rather than individuals hostage.

I have no idea if Ahmadinejad and those who put him in power really believe the Shi'a Twelver doctrine that they can spur the messiah to return by triggering Armageddon. You have to admit, though, that the possibility that they look forward to entering paradise as martyrs would make them a whole lot scarier as a nuclear power than the USSR ever was.

There is hope, though. The Iranian people are not an anti-Western horde. They're an educated and freedom-

loving people for the most part, and reformers there have been begging us for support and sanctions that would weaken the ruling theocracy. Instead, they've just seen the Iranian dictatorship successfully bully the West into impotent submission. This is not a good thing.

We need to understand this and use every means at our disposal, starting with serious and painful international sanctions, to prevent Iran's rulers from becoming the nuclear-armed blackmailers they want to be. Unfortunately, we are hearing demands that we abandon the people of the Middle East who have stood up to Islamo-fascism because they believed us when we said we would support them.

If we retreat precipitously, the price for that betrayal will be paid first in blood and freedom by the Iranian people, the Kurds, the Afghanis, the secular Lebanese, the moderates in Pakistan and the Iraqis themselves. And America's word may never be trusted again. Right now, the pirate Ahmadinejad is clearly more confident about the outcome of the Global War on Terror than we are. That ought to give us pause.

SECURING THE SECOND AMENDMENT

Throughout his career in the U.S. Senate, Fred Thompson won rave reviews from the National Rifle Association for his support for Second Amendment rights for Americans. In the wake of the tragic shooting death of thirty two students at Virginia Tech University in April 2007, he noted that self-protection is a necessary and fundamental right.

SIGNS OF INTELLIGENCE[201]

One of the things that must be going through a lot of peoples' minds now is how one man with two handguns, that he had to reload time and time again, could go from classroom to classroom on the Virginia Tech campus without being stopped. Much of the answer can be found in policies put in place by the university itself.

Virginia, like 39 other states, allows citizens with training and legal permits to carry concealed weapons. That means that Virginians regularly sit in movie theaters and eat in restaurants among armed citizens. They walk, joke and rub shoulders everyday with people who responsibly carry firearms — and are far safer than they would be in San Francisco, Oakland, Detroit, Chicago, New York City, or Washington, D.C., where such permits are difficult or impossible to obtain.

The statistics are clear. Communities that recognize and grant Second Amendment rights to responsible adults have a significantly lower incidence of violent crime than those that do not. More to the point, incarcerated criminals tell criminologists that they consider local gun laws when they decide what sort of crime they will commit, and where they will do so.

Still, there are a lot of people who are just offended by the notion that people can carry guns around. They view everybody, or at least many of us, as potential murderers prevented only by the lack of a convenient weapon. Virginia Tech administrators overrode Virginia state law and threatened to expel or fire anybody who brings a weapon onto campus.

In recent years, however, armed Americans — not on-duty police officers — have successfully prevented a

---

201 The Fred Thompson Report, April 19, 2007. www.abcradio.com.

number of attempted mass murders. Evidence from Israel, where many teachers have weapons and have stopped serious terror attacks, has been documented. Supporting, though contrary, evidence from Great Britain, where strict gun controls have led to violent crime rates far higher than ours, is also common knowledge.

So Virginians asked their legislators to change the university's "concealed carry" policy to exempt people 21 years of age or older who have passed background checks and taken training classes. The university, however, lobbied against that bill, and a top administrator subsequently praised the legislature for blocking the measure.

The logic behind this attitude baffles me, but I suspect it has to do with a basic difference in worldviews. Some people think that power should exist only at the top, and everybody else should rely on "the authorities" for protection.

Despite such attitudes, average Americans have always made up the front line against crime. Through programs like Neighborhood Watch and Amber Alert, we are stopping and catching criminals daily. Normal people tackled "shoe bomber" Richard Reid as he was trying to blow up an airliner. It was a truck driver who found the D.C. snipers. Statistics from the Centers for Disease Control and Prevention show that civilians use firearms to prevent at least a half million crimes annually.

When people capable of performing acts of heroism are discouraged or denied the opportunity, our society is all the poorer. And from the selfless examples of the passengers on Flight 93 on 9/11 to Virginia Tech professor Liviu Librescu, a Holocaust survivor who sacrificed himself to save his students earlier this week, we know what extraordinary acts of heroism ordinary citizens are capable of.

Many *other universities have been swayed by an anti-gun, anti-self defense ideology. I respect their right to hold those views, but I challenge their decision to deny Americans the right to protect themselves on their campuses — and then proudly advertise that fact to any and all.*

Whenever I've seen one of those "Gun-free Zone" signs, especially outside of a school filled with our youngest and most vulnerable citizens, I've always wondered exactly who these signs are directed at. Obviously, they don't mean much to the sort of man who murdered 32 people just a few days ago.

SECURING THE RIGHT TO LIFE

Fred Thompson is definitively "pro-life" on the issue of abortion. During his time in the U.S. Senate he compiled a 100% pro-life voting record. Yet, in the weeks following his announcement that he was "leaving the door open" to a campaign his pro-life record has been critiqued by those pointing to some news reports from his 1994 campaign that classified him as pro-choice. Thompson confesses to being perplexed over the confusion about his position on the issue.

"I have read these accounts [about me being pro-choice] and tried to think back 13 years ago as to what may have given rise to them. Although I don't remember it, I must have said something to someone as I was getting my campaign started that led to a story. Apparently, another story was based upon that story, and then another was based upon *that*, concluding I was pro-choice."[202]

But, he adds: "I was interviewed and rated pro-life by the National Right to Life folks in 1994, and I had a 100 percent voting record on abortion issues while in the Senate."[203]

---

202 Hayes, *"From The Courthouse…"*, *Weekly Standard.*
203 Id.

Darla St. Martin, associate executive director of National Right to Life, supports Thompson on those claims. She traveled to Tennessee in 1994 to meet with him. "I interviewed him and on all of the questions I asked him, he opposed abortion," she told the *American Spectator*'s Philip Klein.[204]

As a Senator, he voted to ban partial birth abortion. He voted against federal funding of abortion. He voted to maintain a ban on abortions at military installations. He says *Roe v. Wade* is bad law and bad science and should be overturned. He would not support a Human Life Amendment to the Constitution.

Planned Parenthood gave him a ZERO rating because of his pro-life voting record. NARAL (National Abortion and Reproductive Rights Action League) gave him an "F" rating when considering potential vice-presidential candidates in 2000.[205]

Thompson clearly had a solid pro-life track record in the U.S. Senate. Ultimately, however, he is motivated on the issue from a personal level, not just a legalistic or moralistic viewpoint. He has said the issue "means more" to him now because he has had two children in recent years. "I have seen the sonograms of my babies."[206]

SECURING AMERICA'S BORDERS

On the issue of illegal immigration, Fred Thompson is not as outspoken as some of the other activists who have led the fight against America's open border policies, like Congressmen Tom Tancredo and Duncan Hunter. But, he has made it clear that he opposes amnesty, in any form, and that securing our borders from a further flood of those who do not enter legally is essential to the security of the United States.

---

204 Id.
205 www.naral.org.
206 Heidi Przybyla and Catherine Dodge, "Thompson Gains Support From Republican Conservatives," Bloomberg.com, April 19, 2007.

SOUTHERN EXPOSURE[207]

We are all very well aware of the fact that we have an illegal-immigration problem in this country. As usual, we avoided the problem for as long as we could and when we couldn't avoid it any longer we were told that, indeed, somewhere between 12 and 20 million people had somehow come into this country unnoticed.

It's like we went overnight from "no problem" to a problem so big that it now defies a good solution. It's become one of those "there are no good choices only less bad choices" that Americans are becoming all too familiar with.

We know that the overwhelming majority of illegals come across the Mexican border. Fortunately, we've got someone who is all too willing to tell us what we should do about it — the president of Mexico Philipe Calderon. President Calderon doesn't think much of our border policies. He criticizes our efforts to secure the border with things such as border fencing. He says that bottle necks at U.S. checkpoints hurt Mexican commerce and force his citizens to migrate illegally in order to make a living (and of course send money back to Mexico). He apparently thinks we should do nothing except make American citizens out of his constituents. Calderon also accused U.S. officials of failing to do enough to stop the flow of drugs in to the United States. Mexican politicians gave President Bush an earful of all of this during his recent trip to Mexico.

I think its time for a little plain talk to the leaders of Mexico. Something like:

---

207 Fred Thompson radio commentary, March 20, 2007, Paul Harvey Show, ABC Radio Networks. www.nationalreview.com.

"*Hey guys, you're our friends and neighbors and we love you but it's time you had a little dose of reality. A sovereign nation loses that status if it cannot secure its own borders and we are going to do whatever is necessary to do so, although our policies won't be as harsh as yours are along your southern border. And criticizing the U.S. for alternately doing too much and too little to stop your illegal activities is not going to set too well with Americans of good will who are trying to figure a way out of the mess that your and our open borders policy has already created.*

My friends, it's also time for a little introspection. Since we all agree that improving Mexico's economy will help with the illegal-immigration problem, you might want to consider your own left-of-center policies. For example, nationalized industries are not known for enhancing economic growth. Just a thought. But here's something even more to the point that you might want to think about: What does it say about the leadership of a country when that country's economy and politics are dependent upon the exportation of its own citizens?"

SECURING
OUR CONSTITUTIONAL RIGHTS

Fred Thompson is an outspoken and passionate supporter of "states rights" as provided under the Constitution of the United States. He was often a lone voice in the U.S. Senate cautioning against the creeping effects of Federalism that overburdens taxpayers and state and local governments alike. As President, he would appoint strict constructionist judges like the man he helped through the confirmation process to the position of Chief Justice, John Roberts.

Fred Thompson's understanding of the Constitution and the rights of Americans guaranteed by that document goes far beyond "sound-bites" and bumper sticker slogans. He has a strong intellectual grasp of the foundations of the American Republic that underscores his passion for the Constitutional principles that our Founding Fathers set forth.

MY RETORT ON TORTS[208]

On April 20, Ramesh Ponnuru penned an article called "Thompson's Tort Trouble."[209] While he referenced my conservative voting, record he took issue with two instances when I voted against "tort reform." He noted my stand on federalist grounds but thinks I must have a mistaken view of Federalism and that conservatives may want to ask me a few hard questions.

This hardly constitutes the stuff of a major dispute, but I would submit that the problem is not so much my mistaken view of Federalism as much as it is his lack of commitment to the principle. This presents conservatives with an opportunity to have a much needed discussion.

First let's discuss the two cases that Mr. Ponnuru cites. The first case involves the issue of "preemption." Congress routinely passes laws and resulting regulations which are in conflict with state laws and regulations. These federal laws do not state whether or not they are intended to preempt the state regulations. Clearly, members of Congress don't want their constituents back home asking why their state authority has been stripped. But Congress can have it both ways. They leave the legislation ambiguous, knowing that the federal courts will more often than not interpret the statute as preempting state law, allowing elected officials in Washington "the federal court did it, I didn't" excuse. This allows for no debate on the issue in Congress, just a decision by that source of so much conservative affection: the federal judiciary.

208 Fred Thompson blog post, April 23, 2007, www.redstate.com.
209 Ramesh Ponnuru, "Thompson's Tort Trouble," www.nationalreview.com, April 20, 2007.

Mr. Ponnuru begins with the assumption that federal preemption of state regulations is inherently a good thing (how Federalist does this sound so far?), because then companies won't have to keep up with all the state laws. I recognize that changes in transportation and communication have created legitimate federal interests where none previously existed. My votes reflect that. But the idea that the commerce clause allows the Feds to regulate anything effecting commerce, no matter how remote, hopefully, is something we can all agree is not acceptable. But I digress. Actually my alleged offense had nothing to do with that. Rather it was the fact that I introduced a bill that essentially said, "Congress must state whether or not the federal legislation is intended to preempt the state regulation." Period.

Mr. Ponnuru not only seems to favor federal preemption in general but thinks that Congress should not be required to acknowledge the fact that it is preempting. Ponnuru says that if my proposal had passed, "the practical result would have been a gold mine for trial lawyers..." (although he doesn't say how).

I disagree. The practical result would have been an open debate as to whether, in any given instance, preemption is a good idea then we would have had a discussion about Federalism. I wonder if Jefferson and Madison thought that we should pick the result we want based upon who we perceive to be the good guys and the bad guys, then get there any way we can?

The other perceived offense on my part had to do with the anti-tobacco bill that came before the Senate in 1998. Senator Lauch Faircloth proposed an amendment that placed a cap on attorneys' fees—fees which had been negotiated between the states and their lawyers. I opposed any fees at all because I opposed the bill. But when the amendment on attorneys' fee came up I opposed it too. Get this: Under the amendment the states would have been required to send the attorneys' bills to the House and Senate Judiciary for approval. As I said on the floor on May 19, 1998, "I did not come to the Senate to review billing records from lawyers in private lawsuits."

For the record, I oppose the federal regulation of any fees negotiated by two competent parties at the state and local level. This goes for lawyers, doctors, butchers, bakers or the occasional candlestick maker. Even if excessive fees offend Congressional sensibilities, there are other remedies that make far more sense than the federal one. In the tobacco case, for example, those who negotiated the attorney's fees had to run for re-election. Also, local courts strike down fees they find excessive. Apparently the absurdity of Patrick Leahy and me (or our staffs) rummaging through records to determine exactly what some second-year lawyer in a Hoboken law firm did to earn their hourly rates is lost on some of my conservative friends. All that matters is that I "sided with the trial lawyers." This is always supposed to end the debate.

This discussion is not an idle exercise. Republicans have struggled in recent years, because they have strayed from basic principles. Federalism is one of those principles. It is something we all give lip service to and then proceed to ignore when it serves our purposes. During my eight years in the Senate, I tried to adhere to this principle. For me it was a lodestar. Not only was it what our founding fathers created – a federal government with limited, enumerated powers with respect for other levels of government, it also provided a basis for a proper analysis of most issues: "Is this something government should be doing? If so, at what level of government?"

As I understood it, states were supposed to be laboratories that would compete with each other, conducting civic experiments according to the wishes of their citizens. The model for federal welfare reform was *the result of that process. States also allow for of diverse viewpoints that exist across the country. There is no reason that Tennesseans and New Yorkers should have to agree on everything (and they don't).*

Those who are in charge of applying the conservative litmus test should wonder why some of their brethren continue to try to federalize more things – especially at a time of embarrassing federal mismanagement and a growing federal bureaucracy. I am afraid that such a test is often based more upon who is favored between two self-serving litigants than upon legal and constitutional principles. Isn't that what we make all the Supreme Court nominees promise not to do?

Adhering to the principles of Federalism is not easy. As one who was on the short end of a couple of 99-1 votes, I can personally attest to it. Federalism sometimes restrains you from doing things you want to do. You have to leave the job to someone else – who may even choose not to do it at all. However, if conservatives abandon this valued principle that limits the federal government, or if we selectively use it as a tool with which to reward our friends and strike our enemies, then we will be doing a disservice to our country as well as the cause of conservatism.

SECURING OUR PROSPERITY

While serving in the U.S. Senate, Fred Thompson was a consistent proponent for lower taxes and a more simplified tax system. He hasn't changed his mind.

CASE CLOSED:
TAX CUTS MEAN GROWTH[210]

It's that time again, and I was thinking of the old joke about paying your taxes with a smile. The punch line is that the IRS doesn't accept smiles. They want your money.

So it's not that funny, but there is reason to smile this tax season. The results of the experiment that began when Congress passed a series of tax-rate cuts in 2001 and 2003 are in. Supporters of those cuts said they would stimulate the economy. Opponents predicted ever-increasing budget deficits and national bankruptcy unless tax rates were increased, especially on the wealthy.

In fact, Treasury statistics show that tax revenues have soared and the budget deficit has been shrinking faster than even the optimists projected. Since the first tax cuts were passed, when I was in the Senate, the budget deficit has been cut in half.

Remarkably, this has happened despite the financial trauma of 9/11 and the cost of the War on Terror. The deficit, compared to the entire economy, is well below the average for the last 35 years and, at this rate, the budget will be in surplus by 2010.

Perhaps the most fascinating thing about this success story is where the increased revenues are coming from. Critics claimed that across-the-board tax cuts were some sort of gift to the rich but, on the contrary, the wealthy are paying a greater percentage of the national bill than ever before.

The richest 1% of Americans now pays 35% of all

---

210 Fred Thompson, April 14, 2007, *Wall Street Journal Opinion Journal,* www.opinionjournal.com.

income taxes. The top 10% pay more taxes than the bottom 60%.

The reason for this outcome is that, because of lower rates, money is being invested in our economy instead of being sheltered from the taxman. Greater investment has created overall economic strength. Job growth is robust, overcoming trouble in the housing sector; and the personal incomes of Americans at every income level are higher than they've ever been.

President John F. Kennedy was an astute proponent of tax cuts and the proposition that lower tax rates produce economic growth. Calvin Coolidge and Ronald Reagan also understood the power of lower tax rates and managed to put through cuts that grew the U.S. economy like Kansas corn. Sadly, we just don't seem able to keep that lesson learned.

Now, as before, politicians are itching to fund their pet projects with the short-term revenue increases that come from tax hikes, ignoring the long-term pain they always cause. Unfortunately, the tax cuts that have produced our record-breaking government revenues and personal incomes will expire soon. Because Congress has failed to make them permanent, we are facing the worst tax hike in our history. Already, worried investors are trying to figure out what the financial landscape will look like in 2011 and beyond.

This issue is particularly important now because massive, unfunded entitlements are coming due as the baby-boom generation retires. We simply cannot afford higher taxes if we want an economy able to bear up under the strain of those obligations. And beyond the issue of our annual federal budget is the nearly $9 trillion national debt that we have not even begun to pay off.

To face these challenges, and any others that we

might encounter in a hazardous world, we need to maintain economic growth and healthy tax revenues. That is why we need to reject taxes that punish rather than reward success. Those who say they want a "more progressive" tax system should be asked one question:

Are you really interested in tax rates that benefit the economy and raise revenue—or are you interested in redistributing income for political reasons?

SECURING OUR FUTURE

On Friday, May 4, 2007, Fred Thompson spoke to a gathering of powerful and influential Republican members of the Lincoln Club in Orange County, California. Some suspected Thompson might actually kick off a campaign from the lectern located in the heart of "Reagan Country." He did not. He did, however, lay out a vision for the future of America that seemed to reflect the thoughts and ambitions for this nation that a candidate for President might spend time expanding upon in the weeks and months leading into 2008.

So we meet again, and I'm honored, because I know we're here for the same reasons: Love of our country and concern for our future.

A lot of Americans have these concerns tonight. They are concerned about the way things are going in our country right now. Some fear we may be in the first stages of decline. We've heard this malaise talk before.

Of course Iraq is a large part of it. Not only is it tough going, but the effort is besieged on all sides. From those playing the most crass kind of politics with it at home to criticism from around the world.

Even at home, as we enjoy the benefits from one of

the best economies we've ever had, people seem
uncertain; they raise concerns about global competition
or a growing economic disparity among our citizens.

These are challenges. But how we react to them is
more important than the challenges themselves. Some
want us, to the extent possible, to withdraw from the
world that presents us with so many problems, in the hope
they will go away. Some would push us towards
protectionist trade policies. Others see a solution in
raising taxes and redistributing the income among our
citizens.

Wrong on all counts. These are defensive, defeatist
policies that have consistently been proven wrong. They
are not what America is all about.

Let's talk about the issues here at home, first. A lot
of folks in Washington suffer from a big misconception
about our economy. They confuse the well-being of our
government with the wealth of our nation. Adam Smith
pointed out the same problem in his day, when many
governments mixed up how much money the king had
with how well-off the country was.

Taxes are necessary. But they don't make the country
any better off. At best they simply move money from the
private sector to the government. But taxes are also a
burden on production, because they discourage people
from working, saving, investing, and taking risks. Some
economists have calculated that today each additional
dollar collected by the government, by raising income-tax
rates, makes the private sector as much as two dollars
worse off.

To me this means one simple thing: tax rates should
be as low as possible. This isn't anything ideological, and
it really isn't some great insight. It's common sense
arithmetic.

That's why the economy booms when taxes are cut. When the Kennedy tax cuts were passed in the 1960s, the economy boomed. When Reagan cut taxes in 1981, we went from economic malaise to a new morning in America. And when George Bush cut taxes in 2001, he took a declining economy he inherited to an economic expansion -- despite 9-11, the NASDAQ bubble and corporate scandals.

The Democrats, of course, want to raise taxes. They only want to target the rich, they say. A word of advice to anyone in the middle class -- don't stand anywhere near that target. Wouldn't it be great if, instead of worrying so much about how to divide the pie, we could work together on how to make the pie bigger?

On globalization -- we're not afraid of it. It works to our benefit. We innovate more and invest in that innovation better than anywhere else in the world. Same thing goes for services, which are increasingly driving our economy. Free trade and market economies have done more for freedom and prosperity than a central planner could ever dream and we're the world's best example of that. So, why do we want to take investment dollars out of growth, and invest it in government?

I'd say cash flow to the government is already going quite well. Over the past year our current tax structure generated record levels of revenue for Washington. In fact it's time to seriously consider what we're getting for our "investment" in government.

For many years, several functions of the federal government have been descending into a sorry state of mismanagement and lack of accountability. I published a 68-page report on government's waste, duplication and inability to carry out some of its basic responsibilities. That was back in 2001 before 9-11, and it got little attention. Now the government's shortcomings are *affecting our national security and are getting a lot of attention.*

The growth of government is not solving these problems; it's causing a lot of them. Every level of new bureaucracy that is created develops a level of bureaucracy beneath it, which creates another one. Pretty soon there is no accountability in the system. A new head of a department or agency comes in from out of town and, after a protracted confirmation fight, wants to spend his or her few years in Washington making great policy and solving national problems, not fighting with their own bureaucrats. So they just let well enough alone. Then you start seeing the results. Departments that can't pass an audit, computer systems that don't work, intelligence breakdowns, people in over their heads.

Yet people in both parties continue to try to federalize and regulate at the national level more and more aspects of American society -- things that have traditionally been handled at the state and local level. We must remember that we have states to serve as policy laboratories for innovation and competition. That's how we got welfare reform. Our system also allows for the diversity of our large country. Our attitude should be, let the federal government do what it is supposed to be doing -- competently. Then maybe we will give it something else to do.

The government could start by securing our nation's borders. A sovereign nation that can't do that is not a sovereign nation. This is secondarily an immigration issue. It's primarily a national security issue. We were told twenty years ago if we produced a comprehensive solution, we'd solve the illegal immigration problem. Twelve million illegals later, we're being told that same thing again. I don't believe most Americans are as concerned about the 12 million that are here as they are about the next 12 million and the next 12 million after *that. I think they're thinking: "Prove you can secure the border and then people of good will can sit down and work out the rest of it, while protecting those folks who play by the rules."*

Speaking of reforms and our economy, there is nothing more urgent than the fate that is awaiting our Social Security and Medicare programs. The good news is that we are living longer. However, we don't have enough young working people to finance these programs from their taxes.

People say the programs are going bankrupt. They won't go bankrupt. Even as these programs sap every dime of the government's revenue, the folks in Washington will raise the taxes necessary to cover the problem. At this rate the federal government is going to wind up as nothing more than a transfer agent -- transferring wealth from one generation to another. It will devastate our economy.

Sometimes I think that I'm the last guy around who still thinks term limits is a good idea. The professionalization of politics saps people's courage. Their desire to keep their job and not upset anybody overrides all else -- even if it hurts the country.

So the entitlement problem gets kicked a little further down the road. This action is based on the premise that our generation is too greedy to help the next generation. I believe just the opposite is true. If grandmom and granddad think that a little sacrifice will help their grandchildren when they get married, try to buy a home or have children, they will respond to a credible call to make that sacrifice -- if they don't think that the sacrifice is going down some government black hole.

I am going to quote my friend, Senator Tom Coburn of Oklahoma. I don't think he'll mind, even though it was a private conversation. He said, "People talk a lot about moral issues, but the greatest moral issue facing our generation is the fact that we are bankrupting the next generation. People talk about wanting to make a difference. Here we could make a difference for generations to come."

It's clear with close numbers in the House and the Senate we need bipartisanship to have any chance at real reform in any of these areas. And there are many responsible people who are willing to try to make it happen. But the level of bipartisanship needed for real progress can only be achieved when politicians perceive that the American people are demanding it. That's why leaders of reform and hopefully our next President, will have a mandate to go directly to the American people with truth and clarity.

These days in Washington, there's an awful lot of talk about the need for conversation -- that we should talk more to our nation's enemies; that we should speak "truth to power." However the speakers are usually turned in the wrong direction. Instead of talking to each other, leaders need to be speaking more to the American people.

The message would be simple: "My friends we have entered a new era. We are going to be tested in many ways, possibly under attack and for a long time. It's time to take stock and be honest with ourselves. We're going to have to do a lot of things better. Here's what we need to do and here's why. I know that, now that you're being called upon, you will do whatever is necessary for the sake of our country and for future generations. You always have."

When the American people respond to that, as I know they will, you will have your bipartisanship.

Section IV: Yeah, But...

...WHAT ABOUT HIS HEALTH?

It takes courage to face cancer, but to go on national television to tell millions of viewers you have it is another thing entirely.

That's exactly what Fred Thompson did on April 11 when he went on national television and talked frankly with Neil Cavuto about his indolent lymphoma.[211]

The cancer is in remission, Fred told Cavuto on Fox News, and it is treatable. The cancer, he said, is "a good kind if you can ever call something like that a good kind."

Fred said that he was diagnosed two-and-a-half years ago after a routine physical.

"I have had no illness from it, or even any symptoms," he said to the television audience. And he told reporters after the show, "My life expectancy should not be affected. I am in remission, and it is very treatable with drugs if treatment is needed in the future — and with no debilitating side effects."

He also made very clear he wouldn't let the idea of cancer slow him down a bit, nor stop his consideration of a race for President. "I wouldn't be doing this if I wasn't satisfied in my own mind as to the nature of it and the fact that not only will I have an average life span, but in the meantime, I will not be affected in any way by it," he said. "Of course nobody knows the future but that has been in the history for almost three years now in terms of no symptoms and no sickness."

Thompson's sudden disclosure of his medical condition was seen by many political experts as clear indication that he was

---

211 *www.foxnews.com/story/0,2933,265601,00.html*

not simply flirting with a presidential race. "It's a clear signal that Fred Thompson is serious about getting into this race," a Republican strategist told the Washington Post at the time. The strategist was cited by the paper as being familiar with Thompson's deliberations who would only speak candidly if granted anonymity.[212]

"He believes that he has to be honest with the American people and that they have to have all the relevant information in order to make a decision," the strategist added. "He wants to see how people respond to this as he gets closer to making the decision about whether to get into the race."[213]

Medical doctor, former Senate Majority Leader and Thompson political insider Bill Frist certainly saw it that way. A few days after Thompson's appearance with Cavuto Frist told the *Weekly Standard* that the existence of the cancer needed to be disclosed before he became an announced candidate for President: "We thought we had to get it out early, in the sense that he's going to be announcing."[214]

Thompson's son Tony also acknowledged the political aspects of the disclosure. "Obviously he needed to put the news out there if he's seriously considering a run to see what the reaction is," he said.[215]

The reaction has been positive, at least based on a flurry of polling conducted following the revelation of Thompson's cancer. Only a few voters nationally, and even fewer identified as Republicans, indicated that the fact he has a mild form of cancer would affect their vote in a presidential primary.

Thompson's medical doctor, Dr. Bruce Cheson, head of hematology at Georgetown University Hospital, said the

212 Dan Balz and David Brown, "Thompson Says Lymphoma Is In Remission," *Washington Post*, April 12, 2007.
213 Id.
214 Hayes, "From the Courthouse...", *Weekly Standard*.
215 Baxter, "'Fred For President,'" *The Sunday Times*.

cancer was initially treated with Rituxan, but that the treatment stopped when the cancer went into remission. Cheson noted that this type of cancer is so slow growing that others who have dealt with it "more often die from natural causes associated with old age rather than from the disease."

Other candidates in the 2008 Presidential field have faced cancer themselves, including Rudy Giuiliani (prostate cancer) and John McCain (skin cancer). John Edwards and his wife Elizabeth announced in March, 2007 that she has a form of bone cancer[216]. She had received successful treatment for breast cancer following the 2004 elections.

As with all candidates, Thompson's cancer will ultimately just be one aspect of "who he is" by the time voters cast their ballots. It will be taken in context with the background, experience and personality that they come to know over the time leading to Election Day. By that time, it is likely to matter very little, if at all.

It is also important to note that Fred Thompson is a trial lawyer, not just on television, but in real life. As a good trial lawyer, he knows that it is always wise to disclose any negative aspects about a case early — and before adversary counsel does so. By getting this story out himself, and early in the process, Thompson signaled that he was truly serious about the race for President.

…ISN'T IT TOO LATE
TO GET INTO THE RACE?

A lot of political experts, some at the encouragement of other candidates for President, are quick to argue that the stage is already set for the 2008 Presidential race and that it is much too late for Thompson to enter at this point.

---

216 *www.cnn.com/2007/POLITICS/03/22/edwards.2008/index.html*

It is easy to point out that other successful candidates have entered the process late in the game. Bill Clinton started his campaign for the 1992 election in October of 1991, merely three months before the first caucus and primaries. George W. Bush began his race in June, 1999. But it is also fair to note that this campaign has begun much earlier than those in the past. It is probably too late for most candidates to enter the race, but Fred Thompson is not "most candidates."

Uncommitted Republican strategist Rich Galen has noted that: "More people will watch Fred Thompson every week on "Law and Order," 20 or 25 million if you include all the versions of it, than will vote in total in the primary season."[217] Millions more heard him filling in for Paul Harvey on radio in March and April, 2007 and with his own regular commentaries for ABC Radio. In fact, Fred gets more television time free (actually he gets paid to be on air) than all the other candidates can afford to purchase.

Is there time to raise the money? According to the first quarter financial reports, Thompson was only $10 million behind Giuiliani and Romney and only $5 million behind McCain. Despite not having raised, or spent, any money yet, Thompson is in the thick of things with second or third place rankings in most national polls and similar results in polling in early primary states.

He will need to raise money quickly, and he can certainly do so. Many of those who have already given the maximum amounts allowed by law to other candidates may also give to him. (Those who have the financial ability to give $2,300 to one political candidate can usually muster up the same amount for another one.) More importantly, Thompson will need to quickly develop a strategy for gathering electronic contributions via the online appeals that Howard Dean put into practice four years ago and which other candidates are already building upon. Thompson's grassroots appeal should

217 Bill Schneider, "Too Late to Get Into the '08 Race?", www.cnn.com, April 9, 2007.

make him very successful in this sort of cost effective and voter-generating effort.

What about getting the political consulting, fundraising and staffing talent on board? Nationally, it should not be very difficult. Particularly as other campaigns may begin to falter once Thompson is an actual candidate. Galen has cited former Bush White House Press Spokesman Ari Fleisher as an example. "He started out as Elizabeth Dole's press secretary [in 1999]. When her campaign floundered and she went out of business, in essence the Bush campaign picked him up as its spokesman, and he ended up the White House spokesman. Consultants are, in essence, fungible."[218]

In 2007, the McCain campaign could provide a lot of talent for Thompson if his campaign continues to stumble and ultimately collapses. It would not be quite as simple as a NASCAR team simply changing drivers, but much of the apparatus of the McCain team might be inherited by Thompson.

The real challenge lies in the early caucus states of Iowa and New Hampshire, where relatively small populations make available political talent a premium. The experienced political talent is crucial because the need to organize volunteers at the precinct and neighborhood level is critical. Thompson's celebrity status will certainly help. The fact that he would fill a perceived ideological void among the Republican field will help even more. But success in those states does require "boots on the ground" and the clock is certainly ticking away for Thompson to recruit and deploy the ground forces needed to win.

However, 2008 has shaped up as an unusual year, not just because of the early start of the fundraising, organizing and campaigning process, but because of the front-loading of the primaries that follow Iowa and New Hampshire. Nearly two

---

218 Id.

dozen states will conduct Republican primary contests on February 5, 2008. Big money and big name recognition are critical to compete in what will, in effect, be a national-type primary on that day. A candidate simply cannot shake enough hands to win Florida, California, Illinois, Missouri, Virginia, Texas, Tennessee, etc. simultaneously. The "personal touch" matters in Iowa and New Hampshire, but it will be impossible after that.

The enthusiasm that a potential Thompson candidacy has already generated all over the country, combined with strong poll numbers nationally and in key states, certainly gives Thompson the opportunity to enter the race during the summer months. It is indeed "late"; but for Thompson, it is not "too late" as long as he gets in with full force by August.

...IS FRED A LAZY CAMPAIGNER?

Most candidates for President of the United States spend years plotting and planning their every move, driven by a passion to win the job that borders, or surpasses in some cases, obsession. That so-called "fire-in-the-belly" is seen as an essential element of winning the White House by many pundits. Many have expressed doubt that Fred Thompson has it.

Nashville political analyst Pat Nolan has said that Thompson has "always been a very effective campaigner but has sometimes lacked focus. Others have described Thompson as endearingly "lazy", but then so was Reagan."[219]

Tony Thompson, Fred's eldest son, has dismissed the concerns: "If he makes the decision to do the job, he will give 110%."[220]

---

219 Baxter, "'Fred For President'", *The Sunday Times*.
220 Id.

Nor does Thompson himself show any concern about the issue when asked about it: "They used to say I moved slowly," he chuckles. "But I move deliberately. I won every one of my races by more than 20 points in a state Clinton carried twice."[221]

There is a lot of frenetic activity in a political campaign, whether it is for city council or President of the United States. Activity, however, does not always equal progress. Efficiency and productivity should be prized, and when you look at the track record of Fred Thompson over his multiple careers, it is hard to argue that he has been less than successful.

Thompson himself has acknowledged that he is not comfortable with the way most people campaign for President. "Going on the road for months at a time, and for all practical purposes, just checking [in] every once in a while; I wouldn't do that. I don't think it has to be done that way. I know people will expect that of everyone — to run frenetically around for years. And I don't do frenetic very well," Thompson told Fox News' Neil Cavuto during an April 11, 1997 interview.

Tom Ingram has watched Fred Thompson work for a long time, and he would caution those who might underestimate him. "If he runs," Ingram has said, "the issue of how hard he will work will be settled pretty quickly on a national stage. He understands the process, and if he gets in, it will be to win."

...WOULD HE BE A GOOD PRESIDENT?

Although Thompson has tremendous credentials and a great deal of expertise in many issues that will be on the "front burner" during the next four years, his lack of "executive level" experience is certainly a valid issue. Every candidate, however, brings a unique set of skills and experiences to the campaign and voters will have to decide which person has what matters most to them in this particular

221 Fund, *"Lights, Camera..."*, *www.opinionjournal.com.*

election.

Former Governors seem to possess the most applicable experience when it comes to the Presidency. Some have fared well in the "big leagues" while others, particularly those who became embroiled in scandal or thought they could micromanage the Federal Government, have not.

The successful track record of those who have been Governors who later win the White House certainly bodes well for former Governors who are in the running. President's Jimmy Carter, Ronald Reagan, Bill Clinton and George W. Bush all spent time as the Chief Executive of their respective states before becoming President. Former Massachusetts Governor Mitt Romney will certainly draw attention to that fact on the campaign trail.[222] Rudy Giuiliani's experience as Mayor of New York is comparable to serving as a Governor, and he will not hesitate to make that point himself.

But previous Presidential elections have not been conducted against the backdrop of international terror. The aftershocks of 9-11, and the persistent threat of the *next* 9-11, make national security experience and expertise more important than ever. As a result, Governors don't have the advantage on the national stage that they once did.

Executive experience is definitely valuable from the standpoint of understanding how to assemble a large team of personnel to "handle the job" once the election is over. Unfortunately, history tells us that those who move from the Governor's office to the White House have a tendency to transplant their entire team to Washington. The advantage is that the "team" is able to hit the ground running and most of the major players know each other well right from the start. But as a group, they may be connected more by their being Texans, or Arkansans, or Georgians, and can tend to be provincial and insular.

---

222 *Former Republican Governors Tommy Thompson, Jim Gilmore, and Mike Huckabee will make a similar case; as will Democrat Governor Bill Richardson.*

President John F. Kennedy may be a better model for assembling a team. He brought in the so-called "whiz kids" of industry and academia that David Halberstam dubbed "The Best and the Brightest" in his 1972 book about the origins of the Vietnam War. Halberstam characterized them as arrogantly insisting on "brilliant policies that defied common sense."

With his varied experiences and connections in Hollywood, Washington, D.C. and the backroads of rural Tennessee, Thompson could recruit a new cadre of the "best and the brightest" with the common sense needed to confront the real-world challenges of today. Because Thompson has never assembled a team for an executive office, it is hard to predict those who will become his key players. But top White House political strategists like Karl Rove, James Carville, Lee Atwater, and others were not household names before their horses won the big race. New names will certainly emerge if Thompson is successful in seeking the White House.

The "Reaganesque" label that is so often applied to Thompson might also be indicative of the type of President he would be. He is clearly a "master communicator," like Reagan. Yet he seems willing to find new ways of communicating with the American people with new technology that was not available to "The Gipper."

"Politics is now one, big 24-hour news cycle, but we seem to spend less time than ever on real substance," he has mused. "What if someone harnessed the Internet and other technologies and insisted on talking about real issues in more depth than consultants would advise? What if they took risks with their race in hopes that the risks to our children could be reduced through building a mandate for good policy?"[223] And what if that use of technology extended beyond the campaign and into the White House?

Finally, the Reagan comparisons seem to go beyond just the

---

223 Fund, "Lights, Camers,...", *www.opinionjournal.com.*

shared background in acting. Many of those within the Reagan inner-circle have thrown their weight behind a Thompson candidacy.[224]

Roger Stone, who was a Reagan campaign strategist, said: "The president Americans want is, in fact, the guy they see on Law and Order: wise, thoughtful, deliberative, confident without the cockiness of George W Bush, urbane yet country. Fred Thompson communicates all those virtues."[225]

Clark Judge, a White House speechwriter for President Reagan, said: "Fred Thompson, like Ronald Reagan, is a man of tremendous substance. There is a sense in the party that none of the candidates is quite 'it'."[226]

Michael Deaver, the Deputy Chief of Staff who helped manage the image of Reagan and is the keeper of the flame today, is quietly assisting the Thompson effort from California.[227]

Bill Kristol, the editor of the conservative *Weekly Standard*, recently noted the comparisons being made between Thompson and Reagan. "Many times I've heard conservative friends consider Thompson's merits (which are real) and then, chuckling, add, 'The last time we nominated an actor, it didn't turn out badly'." Not so badly indeed.

Thompson definitely sees the world as it is, not simply as he wishes it were. He would likely govern as he has lived and worked throughout his lifetime, with straight talk, a sense of humor and humility, a willingness to do what is right even when it is unpopular or means taking on powerful interests, and with a deep and abiding love of his country. Much like Ronald Reagan.

---

224 Tim Shipman, "Reagan's Men Are Backing An – Actor," Sunday Telegraph,
      April 29, 2007.
225 Id.
226 Id.
227 Id.

Conclusion

It is a long and difficult road to January 20, 2009, the date when America's next president ascends the steps of the U.S. Capitol to be sworn in as the 44th President of the United States.

What might unfold on that date is difficult to imagine – let alone predict – 18 months out. But it is a sign of Fred Thompson's name recognition, perceived – and very real – strength of personality, that many people can easily imagine him filling the role of a lifetime, and undertaking the challenging job as America's leader.

Thompson's deep and authoritative voice is well known to millions of viewers of "Law and Order" and millions more familiar with his numerous radio commentaries. His acting background has led to countless feature stories connecting him to another actor who ended up in the White House, Ronald Reagan. But the links to Reagan actually go far beyond a common thread of stage lights and greasepaint.

The clarity of purpose and a common sense conservative approach to complicated issues bond the two men – and with them millions of fellow Americans. Their common ability to communicate effectively is undeniable. But more than a clear-eyed view is the optimism for the future of the country they love that really ties them together. These men share a belief that extraordinarily difficult challenges at home and abroad provide an opportunity to once again show the greatness of America and her people.

Both men's roots were grounded in the early 1960s, when Sen. Barry Goldwater was the conservative standard bearer for Republicans and conservatives. Then, Thompson was a college student and later in law school, where Goldwater's common sense conservatism drew his attention and furthered his interest in policy and politics. At the same time, Ronald Reagan was making his initial forays into politics, embarking on a national speaking tour, discussing ideas and laying the groundwork to become a leader of the conservative movement in America. That speaking tour would launch his political career, first as Governor of California, and later, President of the United States.

Thompson, as well, has been undertaking a similar speaking tour, albeit one that is more spontaneous and immediate. Through his radio and TV appearances, and his increased use of the Internet, Thompson for the past six months has been speaking to, and with, the vast grassroots Republican and conservative quorum across the country. His views on national security, taxes, life issues, the judiciary, pork barrel spending, gun-owner rights, haven't been communicated through the filter of the *New York Times* or the mainstream media. They have been communicated directly to the American people in an entirely unique, 21st century way.

If Thompson chooses to run, it will be in large part due to his ongoing dialogue with the American people, and his ascending leadership as a voice of common sense, conservative ideals of liberty, respect for human dignity and the rule of law that most Americans instinctively support.

What may ultimately seal the deal may be Thompson's inherent humility and sense of purpose for the challenges at hand and ahead. Thompson revealed both during a private meeting with Republican House members, and in an interview with Fox News, when he said that he never had the ambition to be President of the United States. But, he aspired to achieve things for the American people that only a President could achieve.

That is a distinction that can be lost on candidates and often forgotten – or abandoned – by those who take the seat inside the Oval Office. But it is a distinction that many longtime Thompson observers say will not be lost or forgotten by the man with roots in small town Tennessee, who worked his way through college and law school at any job he could find, who has lived his life in every tax bracket, and led a life largely in public view.

The campaign for the White House 2008 has already seen many twists and turns, and there will surely be many more before our nation chooses its next national leader. Regardless of where the campaign may take him, Fred Thompson – through his commonsense approach to issues his optimistic world view and his unique relationship with his fellow Americans – is now a factor in the future of America.

Addendum

In the few weeks since "The Fred Factor" was first published the story has continued to unfold. An exploratory committee was formed, new polls showed Fred Thompson moving to the front of the Republican primary pack, and the impact of his presence looming over the race became increasingly evident. With an official kickoff of a campaign likely to occur in early July, that Thompson presence will be felt even more strongly by the other candidates.

INCREASED VISIBILITY

Fred Thompson made his political "coming out" speech to the Lincoln Club in California on May 4, 2007. It was well received, but many in attendance were under-whelmed and were critical of the fact that Thompson did not address some of the "red meat" issues which are standard fare at such events. A second speech to Connecticut Republicans a week later was also perceived as a bit ragged.

His advisors acknowledged that the initial appearances did not live up to expectations, in part because Thompson was somewhat rusty as a candidate since he had not campaigned since 1996, when he last campaigned for the U.S. Senate. The Thompson team indicated that they planned to sharpen the message for a major address to Republicans in Virginia at their Commonwealth Gala in Richmond on June 2. They did.

At the Virginia dinner, Thompson hit his stride with a speech that mixed warnings about the state of the country with optimism that the American people can overcome the challenges facing them.[1] Thompson showed his gravitas, a charismatic presence, and the ability to connect with an audience. Most importantly, many at the dinner saw him as a

---

1   John Fund, "Right Said Fred," Wall Street Journal Opinion Journal, June 4, 2007. www.opinionjournal.com.

conservative who does not alienate any element within the GOP coalition.

Thompson called on the Virginia Republicans to build "a new coalition" in 2008 that avoids some of the mistakes which led to last November's disaster. "Some of us came to drain the swamp [in Washington] and made partnerships with the alligators," he said, explaining how the GOP Congress ended up tagged as soft on spending.[2]

"Folks, we're a bit down politically right now, but I think we're on the comeback trail, and it's going to start right here," he assured his listeners. "It's like the American people are waiting for us," he continued. "They're waiting for us to remember why we're doing what we're doing, about the ideas that inspired us; to remember who the leaders were that inspired us."[3]

The most enthusiastic response that Thompson received came when he commented on the ongoing debate over illegal immigration. "We are a nation of compassion, a nation of immigrants," Thompson said. "But this is our home, and whether you're a first-generation American, a third-generation American, or a brand newly minted American, this is our home and we get to decide who comes into our home." Thompson received a standing ovation… mid-speech.

Nevertheless, the initial "non-campaign" campaign appearances underlined the difficulties Thompson will face as he makes the transition from potential candidate to actual candidate. Once he emerges "officially," he will attract a greater level of scrutiny from the media and fire from competing campaigns. Some of that has already begun, with claims that Thompson was a "slacker" as a Senator being among the most oft-repeated criticism.

"He didn't have a particularly distinguished Senate career,

2   Id.
3   Id.

though that has never been a bar to anybody else being president," said David Keene, president of the American Conservative Union. "The book on him is he's lazy. I don't know whether that's true or not."[4]

Thompson has shrugged off the "lazy" tag by noting that doing a good job in the U.S. Senate is not just about putting your name on legislation. "There was an awful lot of bad legislation that I helped to stop for one thing," Thompson has said in response to his "thin" legislative record in the Senate.

As to the "lazy" reputation, Thompson has said that it is a rap that will either be revealed or rebuffed on the campaign trail. Indeed, if Thompson is such a lazy campaigner, why are other campaigns so concerned about his emergence as a candidate?

As for his ambivalence about waiting to run for president until age 64, he has joked that voters might appreciate someone "who hasn't lusted for the job since they were student body president." "If a person craves power for the sake of power," Thompson has said, "if he craves the office for the sake of holding the office, he's got his priorities mixed up. It [should be] a desire to do something not be something."[5]

EXPLORATORY EFFORT

The day before his appearance at the Commonwealth Gala in Virginia on June 2, Thompson took a major step towards officially running for President by establishing an exploratory committee to begin fundraising and organizational efforts.[6]

---

4 Susan Page, *"Thompson Wants To Be 2008's Outsider,"* USA Today, May 31, 2007. *www.usatoday.com.*

5 Fund, *"Right Said Fred,"* June 4, 2007.

6 Ironically, the same night Thompson was speaking in Virginia, Mitt Romney was in Tennessee speaking to statewide gathering of Tennessee Republicans at their Statesman's Dinner in Nashville. Romney had been invited as the Keynote Speaker months before Thompson indicated even the slightest interest in a presidential campaign.

Earlier in the week a conference call, which included over 100 Thompson supporters, had actually started the fundraising effort. Each of the individuals, dubbed First Day Founders, was asked to raise at least $50,000 during the weeks leading up to an expected July kick-off for the official campaign.[7] Thompson thanked the supporters for their confidence in him and talked about his reasons for taking this next step toward an official run and answered questions about the issues and campaign strategy. Tom Collamore, a former Reagan and George H.W. Bush administration official (who is considered to be the likely campaign manager), discussed the First Day Founders and their role in this pre-campaign effort.[8] Michael Toner, a former chairman of the FEC who served as the top lawyer on George W. Bush's 2000 campaign before performing the same job at the Republican National Committee, reviewed the laws and regulations governing the testing-the-waters committee.[9] From those participating in the conference call as fundraisers to those participating as managers of the effort, it was clear that Thompson was kicking things off with an A-list team.

Norm Ornstein, a scholar at the American Enterprise Institute and an expert on presidential politics, noted that Thompson was "moving to a whole new level." Ornstein pointed to Thompson's early fundraising efforts as being critical to the success or failure of his campaign. He put the "magic number" for Thompson's first month of fundraising at one million dollars, or more, noting challenges imposed by the campaign limits of $2,300 per person (and $5,000 per PAC).

Thompson's campaign fundraising success exceeded that "magic number" right from the outset. Although the exploratory campaign had intended to raise $5 million within the first month, some campaign insiders have indicated that the sum was actually raised in the first WEEK after the exploratory effort began. In fact, many who were called to donate money to the campaign immediately joined the fundraising team and

---

7   Stephen Hayes, "Testing The Waters," Weekly Standard, May 29, 2007.
8   Id.
9   Id.

begin to solicit donations from others! The Thompson team actually received complaints from some who had not been part of the initial call and who wanted to be added to the list of those willing to raise a minimum of $50,000.

Thompson's initial financial fundraising success was not limited to large donors. On June 5, 2007 Thompson appeared on Fox News' "Hannity and Colmes," just moments after the other Republican presidential candidates debated on CNN in New Hampshire.[10] While on the show he announced a new website, www.imwithfred.com, as his campaign presence on the world wide web. Within forty-eight hours the nascent campaign announced that they already had 29,464 registered supporters, 3,360 donors, and $353,323 in online contributions.[11]

Before the Thompson campaign moved towards a more official status by establishing an exploratory committee, he was already seeing amazing levels of national support being generated by online registrations. The Draft Thompson site, www.draftfred08.com, claimed over 40,000 registrants even before the exploratory committee was announced. Emily Booker, a spokeswoman for the group (and former Thompson Senate staffer), noted that the formation of the exploratory committee had increased traffic to the site and the number of people interested in getting involved in a campaign to elect Fred Thompson.[12]

GEARING UP THE GRASSROOTS

Grassroots support for a "Thompson for President" campaign has been broad-based and seemingly sprang out of nowhere. Tennessee Senator Lamar Alexander

---

10 *Ratings indicate that nearly as many viewers watched Thompson on Hannity and Colmes as watched current GOP candidates debate on CNN. A transcript of Thompson's appearance is available at www.foxnews.com/story/0,2933,278554,00.html.*
11 *Ryan Sager, latestpolitics.com, June 7, 2007.*
    www.latestpolitics.com/blog/2007/06/thompson-web-fundraising-results.html
12 *Brad Schrade, "Thompson Is In The Race," Tennessean, May 31, 2007.*

has said: "The groundswell for Fred is the closest thing to a real, genuine draft that I've seen in my 40 years of politics."

The Thompson candidacy has indeed been driven by a bottom-up groundswell of support. However, the closest advisors to Thompson have not been averse to guiding the movement from the shadows in order to ensure that the "unplanned" plan rolls out most effectively.

Once Thompson "opened the door" to a potential candidacy in early March, 2007, his friends and former staff members were flooded with phone calls from people all over the country asking to be involved and ready to raise money. Public officials from all over the country began issuing endorsements despite the fact that Thompson was not actually a candidate yet.

On April 7, Carl Bearden, the speaker pro tem of the Missouri House of Representatives, sent an email to his colleagues expressing his support for Thompson and encouraging them to do the same. Soon, 60 of the 92 Republicans in the Missouri House had signed a petition backing a Thompson run.[13]

Meanwhile, in Texas, Jerry Patterson, the statewide commissioner of the General Land Office, was circulating a petition encouraging Thompson to run. By late April, he had gotten the signatures of 58 Texas Republican lawmakers. By June, he had recruited 67 of the Texas Republicans to Fred's side, including 59 of the 81 Republicans in the Texas House.[14]

On April 28, an impromptu "Draft Fred" rally was held in a park in Cookeville, Tennessee. Supporters traveled from as far away as Wisconsin, Missouri, Florida, Kansas, and Ohio. One family traveled from Texas to meet their son, a soldier who drove from Fort Bragg after recently returning from Afghanistan. Another supporter was a Canadian man who was

---

13 Stephen Hayes, "The Zero-to-60 Thompson Run," Weekly Standard, June 18, 2007.
14 Id.

in the process of becoming naturalized and hopes to cast his first vote as an American for Fred Thompson. Speaker Carl Bearden of Missouri was also in attendance. Over 500 people turned out on a Saturday afternoon in a tiny town in middle Tennessee.

On May 12, Thompson won the Wisconsin Republican party straw poll with 31 percent of the vote. Six days later, he won a straw poll of Republican delegates to the Georgia Republican convention with 44 percent of the votes cast. (He also has the public support of more than 30 Georgia state legislators.)[15] Showing broad national appeal, he also won a straw poll at a statewide Republican Party dinner in Washington State in early May carrying 50% of the vote.[16]

Whether straw polls and petitions will ultimately translate into fundraising dollars and victories at the ballot box remains to be seen. But Thompson has already created an enviable grassroots organization throughout the country… without even being an announced candidate.

VIDEO OFFENSIVE

Thompson has promised to "break the mold" with his presidential campaign by using new technologies to talk with the voters and to increase their participation in the process. He has specifically cited the internet as a way to "cut through the clutter and go right to the people."

He has already given a few glimpses of how that new style of campaigning might play out in the 2008 election through his blogging, his radio commentaries, and his use of the internet as a fundraising and volunteer recruiting tool. But perhaps the most creative method that the Thompson campaign might employ was revealed in the form of a video response to a debate challenge by filmmaker Michael Moore.

15 Id.
16 *Popular Seattle radio talk host Kirby Wilbur has been an active proponent of a Thompson candidacy.*

In a May 2, 2007 column in the National Review, Thompson had chided Moore for his new film Sicko and the way the documentary favorably compares the health care system in Cuba with the system in the U.S.[17] Moore responded on May 15, 2007 by posting a letter on his website (www.michaelmoore.com) challenging Thompson to a debate on health care.[18] As part of the letter, Moore mentioned Fred's affinity for Cuban cigars (which had been mentioned in recent profile of Thompson) as indicative of his hypocrisy on issues involving Cuba. Moore's challenge to Thompson was picked up by Matt Drudge and immediately posted on his Drudge Report site.[19]

The next morning Thompson's wife, Jeri, pointed out the Drudge item to her husband and suggested he respond and have some fun by putting a video response on the internet. Within about forty minutes two of Thompson's top advisors, Mark Corallo and Ed McFadden, were at his home with a video camera. A couple of hours later a thirty eight second video response to Moore was posted on a newly launched website for videos called Breitbart.tv.

In the video, Thompson sat at his desk in his study where he appeared to be studying his calendar. An unlit Cuban Montecristo cigar was in his mouth.

"You know, I've been looking at my schedule, Michael, and I don't think I have time for you," Thompson drawled while looking into the camera. "But I may be the least of your problems. You know, the next time you're down in Cuba visiting your buddy Castro, you might ask him about another documentary filmmaker. His name is Nicolas Guillen. He did something Castro didn't like, and they put him in a mental institution for several years, giving him devastating electroshock treatment."

17 Fred Thompson, "Paradise Island," National Review, May 2, 2007. www.nationalreview.com.
18 www.michaelmoore.com/words/message/index.php?messageDate=2007-05-15
19 www.drudgereport.com.

"A mental institution, Michael," Thompson concluded. "Might be something you ought to think about."

Within hours the video was being viewed and passed along by hundreds of thousands of people. In fact, the Thompson response was probably seen by more voters than watched the Republican Debate on Fox News in South Carolina the night before the video was released.

It was unconventional and risky, but it worked. And Thompson has acknowledged that continuing to take risks while the "experts" advise caution will be a challenge. "I've got to fight to have the guts enough to follow my own instincts," he has said. "Everybody is going to make mistakes anyway. Things are going to happen. You're going to have good days and bad. You might as well do it your way."[20]

EARLY VOTING IMPACT

In 1976 an unknown Georgia Governor named Jimmy Carter used success in the Iowa Caucus and the New Hampshire Primary to vault to the Democrat Party nomination and ultimately into the White House. Since that time the standard political strategy for a race for the Presidency has involved a lot of time spent in those two states in the years running up to the election. 2008 may require a different strategy.

The 2008 Presidential Primary schedule has never been more front-loaded. About 20 states now have their primary election scheduled for February 5, 2008 – including California, Texas, Tennessee, Virginia, Illinois, and Colorado. Florida has moved its primary up to January 29. That move was made despite the fact that Party rules require it to give up delegates to the two party's conventions. South Carolina will hold a

20 *Susan Page, "Thompson Wants To Be 2008's Outsider," USA Today.*

Democrat Primary on January 29.[21] Candidates who choose to spend their time in Iowa and New Hampshire risk losing ground in larger states that now come so closely on the heels of the "traditional" power states.

The declining impact of Iowa and New Hampshire on the political fortunes of those competing in 2008 is not just a matter of how quickly those other primary elections will follow. Even before the official votes are cast in the Iowa Caucus on January 14, voters in several large states will already be casting their primary votes thanks to "early voting." Voters in Florida, and at least six other states (including Texas, Illinois, Tennessee, California and Colorado), will begin voting before the New Hampshire primary voters head to the polls.[22]

For example, California voters will have the opportunity to cast their ballots starting January 7, a week before the Iowa Caucus. On January 14, Florida voters will begin voting in their "early voting" period -- over a week before the January 22 New Hampshire Primary. While many states continue to restrict voting prior to Election Day except for special circumstances, many of the states that have February 5 primaries provide for unrestricted "early voting."

Candidates who choose to wait until after Iowa or New Hampshire to focus on these other states may be too far behind to catch up, even if they do well in those smaller states. Those with good name recognition and celebrity status, like Fred Thompson, can campaign in the larger states without waiting for a "bounce" from Iowa and New Hampshire.[23]

---

21 South Carolina Republicans have set their date for February 2, but have indicated a desire to be among the first in the South. With Florida moving to January 29 they may yet move to that date as well.

22 For a thorough analysis of the early voting schedule see: Christopher Cooper, "Early Voting May Clip Iowa's Role," The Wall Street Journal, May 22, 2007.

23 Thompson has clearly targeted Florida. The third-ranking Republican in the State House, Adam Putnam, has signed on with Thompson. George P. Bush, the nephew of President George W. Bush and son of former Florida Governor Jeb Bush has also joined the Thompson team. Stephen Hayes, "Thompson Targets Florida," Weekly Standard, June 4, 2007.

MOVING TOWARDS
FRONT-RUNNER STATUS

As Fred Thompson moved closer and closer to an actual campaign kickoff a series of polls in mid-June underscored the impact he was already having on the race. A June 5, 2007 Rasmussen Reports poll of Republican voters nationwide showed Rudy Giuliani leading the pack with 23%, Thompson in second with 17%, Romney in third with 15% and McCain narrowly behind in with 14%.

A week later, having established an exploratory committee and with a flurry of national media coverage, the same poll showed Thompson moving into a tie with Giuliani for first place at 24% each, and Romney and McCain slipping into a tie at 11% each.[24] McCain has seen his support in this particular poll slip to nearly half of what it was in January.

Finally, on June19, Thompson actually moved into first place in the Rasmussen Reports poll with a narrow one point lead over Giuliani. His 28-27% lead over Giuliani represented a four point bounce in the poll in a single week. McCain and Romney both trailed the two front-runners, tied at 10% each.[25]

Further evidence of the Republican race becoming a two-man contest between Thompson and Giuliani came in a June 11, 2007 Los Angeles Times/Bloomberg poll which showed Thompson moving into a solid second place in the Republican primary battle while Giuliani remained in first place. The LA Times/Bloomberg poll had Giuliani at 27%, Thompson at 21%, McCain 12%, and Romney with 10%.[26]

The impact of Fred Thompson's entry into the race has been most strongly felt by John McCain, who has slipped from first or second in most national polls to a third or fourth

---

24 *www.rasmussenreports.com.*
25 *Rasmussen Reports, June 19, 2007, www.rasmussenreports.com.*
26 *http://www.latimes.com/media/acrobat/2007-06/30445335.pdf*

position. In South Carolina, for example, McCain once enjoyed front-runner status but has seen Thompson move into the top spot in the most recent Mason-Dixon Poll while he has slipped to fourth place with support from just 7% of South Carolina's likely Republican Primary voters.[27]   If McCain's fundraising numbers slip as much as his poll numbers in the coming months he will not be a candidate by the time the Iowa Caucus and New Hampshire Primary take place.

Poll numbers will shift up and down during the months ahead. They are merely snapshots of public opinion that can change quickly and sometimes inexplicably. But the fact that Fred Thompson has emerged as a leading contender for the Republican nomination BEFORE he even officially announced, campaigned rigorously, or raised money is yet another testament to the potential impact of the Fred Factor on the 2008 Presidential Race. As he drops the "potential" tag and becomes an "actual" candidate the story will begin in earnest.

---

[27]   *Mason-Dixon Poll, June 13-15, 2007, www.mason-dixon.com.*